MODERNIZATION OF RUSSIA
UNDER PETER I AND CATHERINE II

MAJOR ISSUES IN HISTORY

Editor
C. WARREN HOLLISTER
University of California, Santa Barbara

MODERNIZATION OF RUSSIA UNDER PETER I AND CATHERINE II

EDITED BY

Basil Dmytryshyn

Portland State University

John Wiley & Sons, Inc.

New York • London • Sydney • Toronto

Cover Illustration: *Russian Folk Illustrations,* Rovinski, 1881

Library of Congress Cataloging in Publication Data:

Dmytryshyn, Basil, 1925-   comp.
    Modernization of Russia under Peter I and Catherine II.
    (Major issues in history)

1. Russia—History—Peter I, 1689–1725
2. Russia—History—Catherine II, 1762–1796.
3. Peter I, the Great, Emperor of Russia, 1672–1725.
4. Catherine II. Empress of Russia, 1729–1796
I. Title.

DK133.D58   947′.05   73-16358
ISBN 0-471-21635-6
ISBN 0-471-21636-4 (pbk.)
Printed in the United States of America

10 9 8 7 6 5 4 3 2 1

To the Memory of My Father

SERIES PREFACE

The reading program in a history survey course traditionally has consisted of a large two-volume textbook and, perhaps, a book of readings. This simple reading program requires few decisions and little imagination on the instructor's part, and tends to encourage in the student the virtue of careful memorization. Such programs are by no means things of the past, but they certainly do not represent the wave of the future.

The reading program in survey courses at many colleges and universities today is far more complex. At the risk of over-simplification, and allowing for many exceptions and overlaps, it can be divided into four categories: (1) textbook, (2) original source readings, (3) specialized historical essays and interpretive studies, and (4) historical problems.

After obtaining an overview of the course subject matter (textbook), sampling the original sources, and being exposed to selective examples of excellent modern historical writing (historical essays), the student can turn to the crucial task of weighing various possible interpretations of major historical issues. It is at this point that memory gives way to creative critical thought. The "problems approach," in other words, is the intellectual climax of a thoughtfully conceived reading program and is, indeed, the most characteristic of all approaches to historical pedagogy among the newer generation of college and university teachers.

The historical problems books currently available are many and varied. Why add to this information explosion? Because the Wiley Major Issues Series constitutes an endeavor to produce something new that will respond to pedagogical needs thus far unmet. First, it is a series of individual volumes—one per problem. Many good teachers would much prefer to select their own historical issues rather than be tied to an inflexible sequence of issues imposed by a publisher and bound together between two covers. Second, the Wiley Major Issues Series is based on the idea of approaching the significant problems of history through a deft interweaving of primary sources and secondary analysis, fused together by the skill of a scholar-editor. It is felt that the essence of a historical issue cannot be satisfactorily probed either by placing a body of undigested source materials into the hands of inexperienced students or by limiting these students to the controversial literature of modern scholars who debate the meaning of sources the student never sees. This series approaches historical problems by exposing students to both the finest historical thinking on the issue and some of the evidence on which this thinking is based. This synthetic approach should prove far more fruitful than either the raw-source approach or the exclusively second-hand approach, for it combines the advantages—and avoids the serious disadvantages—of both.

Finally, the editors of the individual volumes in the Major Issues Series have been chosen from among the ablest scholars in their fields. Rather than faceless referees, they are historians who know their issues from the inside and, in most instances, have themselves contributed significantly to the relevant scholarly literature. It has been the editorial policy of this series to permit the editor-scholars of the individual volumes the widest possible latitude both in formulating their topics and in organizing their materials. Their scholarly competence has been unquestioningly respected; they have been encouraged to approach the problems as they see fit. The titles and themes of the series volumes have been suggested in nearly every case by the scholar-editors themselves. The criteria have been (1) that the issue be of relevance to undergraduate lecture courses in history, and (2) that it be an issue which the scholar-editor knows thoroughly and in which he has done creative work. And, in general, the second criterion has been given precedence over the first. In short, the question "What are the significant historical issues today?" has been answered not by general editors or sales departments but by the scholar-teachers who are responsible for these volumes.

University of California,   *C. Warren Hollister*
Santa Barbara

CONTENTS

PART TWO

Modernization of Russia Under Catherine II

MODERNIZATION OF RUSSIA
UNDER PETER I AND CATHERINE II

INTRODUCTION

There is a general consensus in historical literature that the reigns of Peter I (1682–1725) and Catherine II (1762–1796) exerted profound influence on the course of Russian and European history. This observation is immediately apparent when one studies the bulky content of their decrees, instructions, and letters, and when one examines the voluminous, multilingual, literature (monographic and periodical) about their reigns that has appeared during the past two centuries. Based on its content, the existing literature can be divided into two broad categories: one that praises domestic and foreign policies of the two monarchs for making possible the transformation of Russia from a relatively weak and backward country into a powerful and modern European nation; and another that deplores that transformation on account of the methods used to achieve it and the price the Russian people had to pay for it.

What were some of the major manifestations of that transformation that some scholars interchangeably call modernization or Westernization? The most striking aspects appeared at Court. This is not at all surprising since the Court initiated and spearheaded all changes, not only of the physical surroundings but of customs, habits, tastes, and the entire way of life. The transformation began during the reign of Peter I. Before his time the Court of Russia had very strong Byzantine–Oriental features. In outward appearance the tsar resembled a composite of a Chinese emperor, a Persian shah, and a Byzantine patriarch. Because of his close association with the Orthodox Church, life at Court was both religious and mysterious. The tsar's palace in the Kremlin was surrounded by churches; religious services were conducted several times a day; many of the tsar's top advisors were clergymen; he wore clothing made from the same material as that worn by the patriarch; and, like the patriarch, he was carried during all ceremonial processions.

Peter I changed all that. He moved the Court from Moscow to Petersburg (which he had ordered to be built), donned a military uniform, supplanted religious advisors with military men,

1

and replaced religious ceremonies with concerts, masquerades, dances, hunting parties, fireworks displays, theater, and other worldly entertainments. Women, who until this time had been forced to lead a secluded life, were allowed to take their proper place in public and politics and became the center of affection and attraction. In the course of the eighteenth century four women became empresses of Russia. Most of the buildings of the new capital were designed and decorated by West European architects and artists, and, during the reign of Catherine II, St. Petersburg virtually replaced Versailles as the cultural and entertainment center of Europe.

The example of a life-style set by the Court was imitated by rich nobles, who began to build their own palaces in towns and on their estates. Like the palaces of the tsar, the palaces of the nobles were "modern" and "European." They were surrounded by elaborate parks and gardens, which abounded in plantings, fountains, statuaries, bird houses, and other paraphernalia. Each palace, too, was furnished and decorated in the latest elegant fashion. The departure was quite revolutionary because, generally speaking, before the eighteenth century the home of a Russian nobleman differed little from the home of an ordinary person. Now, however, benches along the walls gave way to chairs and sofas; walls were decorated with expensive paintings and ornate mirrors; and all rooms were well provided with delicate furniture, porcelain, and bronze statuettes, and other dust-collecting objects. The latter were either imported from European dealers or were created on the spot by foreign or native craftsmen.

These and other innovations in the living environment were accompanied by a drastic revolution in clothing. Until the eighteenth century the style of a Russian nobleman's clothing resembled a combination of that of a Mandarin official and a medieval monk. Here, too, Peter I ordered a drastic change. He forced all nobles to shave their faces and to wear the latest style of European clothing. The Court carried the extravagance in clothing to extreme proportions. Peter I's daughter, Elizabeth (after she became empress), assembled thousands of dresses, stockings, shoes, hats, and other "necessities." The wardrobe of Catherine II was both extensive and expensive. Since most nobles imitated the style set by the Court, they, like their French counterparts, brought financial ruin upon themselves.

Closely tied with the modernization of Court life and life of the upper echelons of society was the transformation of Russia's armed forces. Before Peter I's time the Russian army might best be described as a massive human wave. It had incompetent leadership and was equipped with diverse and obsolete weapons. It won victories not as a result of skilled tactics or strategy but by mass assaults, regardless of the human cost. With the aid of foreign specialists Peter I gave the Russian army new organization, new uniforms, new standardized weapons, and a new purpose. From its inception the new army became a regular army, trained and led by educated professional soldiers. Its effectiveness was tested at the battle of Poltava (1709), and it soon acquired fame for endurance, discipline, determination, and bravery. As the most essential instrument of power and conquest the new army also received preferential treatment and consideration. In the course of the eighteenth century the modernized army won many battles for Russia, not only against the Swedes and the Ottoman Turks, but against the Poles, the French, and the Prussians. It was her spectacular military performance that propelled Russia to the top of the European power system. It was also that performance that gained for Russia enormous and valuable territories in Europe and Asia.

If the Russian army served as the right hand of the tsar's power, the navy functioned as the left hand. The navy was Peter I's creation. To realize his lifelong dream he bought some ships abroad, built others at home, invited experienced European sailors to come to Russia, and forced thousands of young Russians into schools (foreign and domestic) to study navigation and related subjects. These preliminaries soon brought rich dividends. Between 1713 and 1720, the Russian navy won several battles against the Swedes in the Baltic, and a fleet was built in the Caspian and the Azov Seas to protect as well as to expand Russian interests in that region. By Peter I's death in 1725, Russia had emerged as a naval power.

Peter I's immediate successors neglected somewhat the needs of the navy, but with the ascension of Catherine II in 1762 that

neglect ceased. To improve naval sciences Catherine II founded the
Marine Cadet Corps and the Marine Engineering School. She
ordered the modernization of naval armaments, dispatched a
fleet from the Baltic to the Mediterranean to fight the Ottoman
Turks, and ordered construction of harbor facilities and ship
yards at Taganrog, Kherson, and Sevastopol. Upon her death in
1796, the Russian navy, commanded by Russian and European
captains, was the second largest fleet in the world (after England) —a preeminence it regained only after World War II.

Another vital field that underwent drastic modernization was
diplomacy. Russia had long been a large, resourceful, and populous state, but because of her isolation she exerted little influence
on European affairs prior to Peter I's reign. Her ambassadors
were awkward and unfamiliar with customs and European languages, and their appearance and behavior were often a source
of amusement and disbelief. Peter I introduced a new direction
into Russian diplomacy. He engaged in the Russian diplomatic
service many skilled foreign adventurers, dispatched permanent
diplomatic observers to strategic locations to report on vital developments, inaugurated a policy of marriage alliances, and, after his victories over Sweden, forced Europe to accept Russia as a
full partner of Europe. During her reign, Catherine II changed
that partnership to virtual domination of Europe. German by
birth, Russian by choice, French in spirit, and Machiavellian by
training, Catherine II, and her ambassadors, became the master
of diplomatic intrigue and trade. They partitioned Poland
(1772–1795), dismembered the Ottoman Empire (1768–1792),
interferred into and "mediated" the affairs of the Holy Roman Empire (1778–1779), openly challenged the supremacy of
the British (1780), spearheaded the movement to contain revolutionary France (after 1789), and conceived other alliances aimed
at enhancing Russia's position in European affairs.

Next to diplomacy, the eighteenth-century Russians made the
most outstanding breakthrough in culture. Until Peter I's time
Russian culture was under the domination of the Orthodox
Church. The Russians computed time according to the Byzantine
calendar; they used Church-Slavonic as the literary language;
and architecture and painting were Church oriented. Peter I altered all that. He introduced the Julian Calendar, modernized

the alphabet, started a newspaper and a theater, moved literature from the service of the Church to the service of the state, society, and science; established secular schools; and, with the aid of many West Europeans (Germans, Dutch, and Englishmen), opened Russia to Western secular ideas, learning, and influences. The trend encountered opposition but it became irreversible. Russia began to produce what became a whole galaxy of native literary figures, explorers, publicists, scientists, architects, painters, historians, journalists, and other men of culture and learning. The real blossoming of this achievement came during the reign of Catherine II, who is considered by many to be the most enlightened of all the despots and a mistress of many trades.

The foregoing selected samples, which by no means exhaust the subject, point to two significant conclusions. The first is that during their reigns Peter I and Catherine II introduced many important innovations that modernized the life-style of the Court and of the nobility, the organization of the armed forces and of the state administrative apparatus, the conduct of diplomacy, education, and similar areas of activity. Thanks to these innovations, in the course of the eighteenth century Russia acquired a firm foundation for its transformation from a relatively weak and backward country into a mighty, modern nation of Europe.

The second striking feature of these modernizing innovations is their limited scope. Neither Peter I nor Catherine II, for example, introduced any change affecting the nature or the scope of their power. It remained autocratic and absolute and was based on divine right. Similarly, neither monarch introduced any innovation aimed at improving or modernizing the lives of the country's lower strata of society. On the contrary, during their reigns the inhuman institution of medieval serfdom became almost universal and was extended to many areas that had never before experienced it.

The list of such contradictions is very long and shows that the modernizing efforts of Peter I and Catherine II were narrow, uneven, and imbalanced, with the result that at the end of the eighteenth century Imperial Russia was a mixture of clashing contrasts. It was the most resourceful country in the world, but its agriculture, industry, and the communications system were among the most primitive. It had good schools for a privileged few, but illiteracy was the way of life for the overwhelming majority. It had a small class of cultured nobles who lived in sumptuous villas, who wore modern clothing, who discussed the latest ideas of Western Europe, and who were fluent in French, German, and English, but it also had millions of illiterate and superstitious peasants who lived in the most horrible filth and poverty. This paradox troubled contemporaries as well as historians and has given rise to many conflicting interpretations of the reigns of Peter I and Catherine II.

The selections that follow are typical examples of the existing diversity of views. They have been selected not because I necessarily agree with their views, but because they may provide the reader with valuable keys to a fair and accurate understanding of the reigns of Peter I and Catherine II—Imperial Russia's most controversial monarchs.

PART I

Modernization of Russia Under Peter I

1   *Modernization by Administrative Decrees*

In his efforts to modernize Russia, Peter I employed a variety of methods. In some instances he himself set the necessary example; in others he resorted to terror; in still others he tried persuasion and rewards; and throughout his reign he extensively employed administrative decrees. Decrees seem to have been the most lasting of these methods since they outlived him, his terror, and his rewards. The introduction of the Julian calendar, for example, continued in official use in Russia until February, 1918; the Table of Ranks was in force until 1917, while the academy he conceived exists to the present day. The few samples of Peter I's decrees given below form only a very small part of his modernization efforts. Many have been published, but a great deal still remains to be made public.

SOURCES. Items in this selection came from the following sources: (a) *Polnoe Sobranie Zakonov Russkoi Imperii* . . . [Complete Collection of the Laws of the Russian Empire], 1st Series. Vol. 3, No. 1736; (b) *Ibid.*, Vol. 5, No. 2778; (c) *Ibid.*, Vol. 5, No. 2979; (d) *Ibid.*, Vol. 5, No. 2999; (e) *Pisma i bumagi imperatora Petra Velikogo* [Letters and Papers of Emperor Peter the Great] (St. Petersburg: 1887), Vol. I, pp. 117–118; (f) *Polnoe Sobranie Zakonov* . . . 1st Series, Vol. 6, No. 3693; (g) . P. Pekarskii, *Nauka i literatura v Rossii pri Petre Velikom* [Science and Literature Under Peter the Great] (St. Petersburg: 1862), Vol. 1, pp. 532–533; and (h) *Polnoe Sobranie Zakonov* . . . 1st Series. Vol. 7, No. 4443. All items in this selection were translated by Basil Dmytryshyn.

(A) A DECREE ON A NEW CALENDAR, DECEMBER 20, 1699

The Great Sovereign has ordered it declared: the Great Sovereign knows that many European Christian countries as well as Slavic peoples are in complete accord with our Eastern Orthodox Church, namely: Wallachians, Moldavians, Serbs, Dalmatians, Bulgars, and subjects of our Great Sovereign, the Cherkessy [Ukrainians] and all Greeks from whom we accepted our Orthodox faith—all these peoples number their years from eight days after the birth of Christ, that is from January 1, and not from the creation of the world. There is a great difference in those two calendars. This year is 1699 since the birth of Christ, and on January 1 it will be 1700 as well as a new century. To celebrate this happy and opportune occasion, the Great Sovereign has ordered that henceforth all government administrative departments and fortresses in all their official business use the new calendar beginning January 1, 1700. To commemorate this happy beginning and the new century, in the capital city of Moscow, after a solemn prayer in churches and private dwellings, all major streets, homes of important people, and homes of distinguished religious and civil servants should be decorated with trees, pine, and fir branches similar to the decoration of the Merchant Palace or the Pharmacy Building—or as best as one knows how to decorate his place and gates. Poor people should put up at least one tree, or a branch on their gates or on their apartment [doors]. These decorations are to remain from January 1 to January 7, 1700. As a sign of happiness on January 1, friends should greet each other and the New Year and the new century as follows: when the Red Square will be lighted and shooting will begin—followed by that at the homes of boyars, courtiers, and important officials of the tsar, military and merchant classes —everyone who has a musket or any other fire arm should either salute thrice or shoot several rockets or as many as he has. . . .

(B) A DECREE ON COMPULSORY EDUCATION OF THE RUSSIAN NOBILITY, FEBRUARY 28, 1714

The Great Sovereign has decreed: in all *gubernias* children between the ages of ten and fifteen of the nobility, of government clerks, and of lesser officials, except those of freeholders, must be taught mathematics and some geometry. Toward that end, students should be sent from mathematical schools [as teachers], several into each *gubernia,* to prelates and to renowned monasteries to establish schools. During their instruction these teachers should be given food and financial remuneration of three *altyns* and two *dengas*[1] per day from *gubernia* revenues set aside for that purpose by personal orders of His Imperial Majesty. No fees should be collected from students. When they have mastered the material, they should then be given certificates written in their own handwriting. When the students are released they ought to pay one ruble each for their training. Without these certificates they should not be allowed to marry nor receive marriage certificates.

(C) A DECREE ON THE ESTABLISHMENT OF SECULAR SCHOOLS, JANUARY 18, 1716

The Great Sovereign has decreed: By order of His personal decree, in every gubernia children of all government officials, except those of nobles, must be taught numbers and some aspects of geometry in accordance with His Majesty's previous ukazes of February 28, 1714, and December 28, 1715. To achieve that goal, those students in the school [supervised by] Admiral Count Apraxin, who have mastered geography and geometry, should be selected and at least two dispatched to each gubernia. They should teach in the gubernia schools in accordance with stipulations provided by an earlier ukaz of His Imperial Majesty. His Imperial Majesty has forwarded ukazes about this matter to Admiral Apraxin and to all governors. The ukaz to the Admiral states that the would-be teachers should be sent from the Admiralty Office in Moscow to the Office of the Senate, and from there to [their assignments in] the gubernias.

---

[1] One *altyn* equaled six *dengas,* or three copecks; one *denga* equaled one-half copeck.

(D) PETER I's ORDER SENDING YOUNG RUSSIANS ABROAD TO STUDY NAVIGATION, MARCH 2, 1716

We have received news from Italy that in Venice they wish to accept our [people] into naval service training; today the French have also responded saying that they too will accept our [trainees]. Consequently, select immediately in the Petersburg schools children of well-to-do nobles, bring them to Reval, and place them aboard ships. There should be sixty of them. Send twenty to Venice, twenty to France, and twenty to England. Should they be unable to reach Reval in time, and should their ships sail away, then send them to Riga aboard the crafts *Diana* and *Natalia,* and from there by stage coach to Memel, and from Memel by hired coaches to Mecklenburg, where I should be at the time.

(E) AN INSTRUCTION TO RUSSIAN STUDENTS ABROAD STUDYING NAVIGATION

1. Learn [how to draw] plans and charts and how to use the compass and other naval indicators.

2. [Learn] how to navigate a vessel in battle as well as in a simple maneuver, and learn how to use all appropriate tools and instruments; namely, sails, ropes, and oars, and the like matters, on row boats and other vessels.

3. Discover as much as possible how to put ships to sea during a naval battle. Those who cannot succeed in this effort must diligently ascertain what action should be taken by the vessels that do and those that do not put to sea during such a situation [naval battle]. Obtain from [foreign] naval officers written statements, bearing their signatures and seals, of how adequately you [Russian students] are prepared for [naval] duties.

4. If, upon his return, anyone wishes to receive [from the Tsar] greater favors for himself, he should learn, in addition to the above enumerated instructions, how to construct those vessels aboard which he would like to demonstrate his skills.

5. Upon his return to Moscow, every [foreign-trained Russian] should bring with him at his own expense, for which he

will later be reimbursed, at least two experienced masters of naval science. They [the returnees] will be assigned soldiers, one soldier per returnee, to teach them [what they have learned abroad]. And if they do not wish to accept soldiers they may teach their acquaintances or their own people. The treasury will pay for transportation and maintenance of soldiers. And if anyone other than soldiers learns [the art of navigation] the treasury will pay 100 rubles for the maintenance of every such individual. . . .

(F) A DECREE ON THE GATHERING OF HISTORICAL MATERIAL, DECEMBER 20, 1720

The Great Sovereign has decreed: Examine, and gather in all monasteries located within the Russian Empire, all ancient charters and other unusual original letters, as well as historical books, manuscripts, and published works that are still used or [whose existence] may be known. In accordance with the Great Sovereign's ukaz, the Governing Senate has decreed the following: Governors, Vice-Governors, and voevodes are hereby ordered to examine and record in all dioceses, monasteries, and cathedrals all ancient charters and other unusual original letters as well as historical manuscripts and published books, and send the recorded books to the Senate.

(G) PETER I's ACCEPTANCE OF MEMBERSHIP IN THE ROYAL FRENCH ACADEMY, FEBRUARY 11, 1721

We, Peter I, by God's Grace, Tsar and Autocrat of All Russia, etc., etc., etc.

We hereby send Our gracious greetings to the Royal French Academy.

We have indeed been very pleased that you have selected Us as a member of your association. We are very delighted that you have honored Us in this way, and We would like to assure you that We shall accept the position you have given Us with great pleasure, and that it is Our fervent wish to apply Ourself assiduously in order to contribute as much as possible to science, and thereby to demonstrate that We are a worthy member of your association. We have instructed Our chief physician, Blumenrost, to inform you from time to time about new developments in Our states and territories, and to receive from you news about developments in the Academy. It would please Us greatly if you would correspond with him, and if, from time to time, you would inform him about new discoveries by the Academy.

Until now no one has prepared any reliable map of the Caspian Sea. We sent to that sea experienced seamen to survey it, and to prepare an accurate map of it. After two years of work they completed that assignment. We are sending that map to the Academy to commemorate Our name, and We hope that you will accept the new and precise map [of the Caspian Sea]. Finally, we trust that Our chief physician will convey more in writing, and that Our chief librarian will convey more orally.

Given in St. Petersburg, February 11, 1721.

Affectionately yours,
[Peter I]

(H) A DECREE ON THE FOUNDING OF THE ACADEMY, JANUARY 28, 1724

His Imperial Majesty decreed the establishment of an academy, wherein languages as well as other sciences and important arts could be taught, and where books could be translated. On January 22, [1724], during his stay in the Winter Palace, His Majesty approved the project for the Academy, and with his own hand signed a decree that stipulates that the Academy's budget of 24,912 rubles annually should come from revenues from custom dues and export-import license fees collected in the following cities: Narva, Dorpat, Pernov and Arensburg. . . .

Usually two kinds of institutions are used in organizing arts and sciences. One is known as a University; the other as an Academy or society of arts and sciences.

1. A University is an association of learned individuals who teach the young people the development of such distinguished sciences as theology and jurisprudence (the legal skill), and

medicine and philosophy. An Academy, on the other hand, is an association of learned and skilled people who not only know their subjects to the same degree [as their counterparts in the University] but who, in addition, improve and develop them through research and inventions. They have no obligation to teach others.

2. While the Academy consists of the same scientific disciplines and has the same members as the University, these two institutions, in other states, have no connection between themselves in training many other well-qualified people who could organize different societies. This is done to prevent interference into the activity of the Academy, whose sole task is to improve arts and sciences through theoretical research that would benefit professors as well as students of universities. Freed from the pressure of research, universities can concentrate on educating the young people.

3. Now that an institution aimed at the cultivation of arts and sciences is to be chartered in Russia, there is no need to follow the practice that is accepted in other states. It is essential to take into account the existing circumstances of this state [Russia], consider [the quality of Russian] teachers and students, and organize such an institution that would not only immediately increase the glory of this [Russian] state through the development of sciences, but would also, through teaching and dissemination [of knowledge], benefit the people [of Russia] in the future.

4. These two aims will not be realized if the Academy of Sciences alone is chartered, because while the Academy may try to promote and disseminate arts and sciences, these will not spread among the people. The establishment of a university will do even less, simply because there are no elementary schools, gymnasia, or seminaries [in Russia] where young people could learn the fundamentals before studying more advanced subjects [at the University] to make themselves useful. It is therefore inconceivable that under these circumstances a university would be of some value [to Russia].

5. Consequently what is needed most [in Russia] is the establishment of an institution that would consist of the most learned people, who, in turn, would be willing: (a) to promote and perfect the sciences while at the same time, wherever possible, be

willing (b) to give public instruction to young people (if they feel the latter are qualified) and (c) instruct some people individually so that they in turn could train young people [of Russia] in the fundamental principles of all sciences.

6. As a result, and with only slight modifications, one institution will perform as great a service [in Russia] as the three institutions do in other states. . . .

7. Because the organization of this Academy is similar to that of Paris (except for this difference and advantage that the Russian Academy is also to do what a university and college are doing [in Paris]), I think that this institution can and should easily be called an Academy. Disciplines which can be organized in this Academy can easily be grouped in three basic divisions: The first division is to consist of mathematical and related sciences; the second of physics; and the third of humanities, history and law. . . .

2   *Contemporary Foreign*
Assessments of Peter I's Modernization of Russia

Peter I's efforts to modernize Russia left a deep imprint not only on Russians but on West Europeans as well. Of the latter, thousands became involved directly in the modernization process as teachers, officers, engineers, administrators, and overseers of one kind or another. Many foreigners who either took an active part or who witnessed the great transformation of the country left interesting accounts of their impressions. The first account in this selection is by an Englishman named John Perry, a hydraul-

SOURCE. John Perry, *The State of Russia Under the Present Czar* . . . (London: 1716), pp. 185–187, 194–202, 220–221, 234–238, and 260–263; Friedrich Christian Weber, *The Present State of Russia* . . . (London: 1723), Vol. I, pp. 14–20, 47–50, 128–129, 147–150, and 188–190; and Johann G. Vockerodt, "Rossiia pri Petre Velikom" [Russia Under Peter the Great], *Chteniia v Imperatorskom Obshchestve Istorii* . . ., II, (1874), pp. 4–5, 17, 30–31, 50–51, and 100–106. Spellings, especially of proper names, have been modernized in the works by Perry and Weber. Translation of Vockerodt's account is by Basil Dmytryshyn.

*ic engineer, who spent fourteen years (1698–1712) in Russia at
Peter I's request. The second selection is by Friedrich Christian
Weber, a Dutch Minister to Russia, who lived there from 1714
to 1720. The third account is by Johann G. Vockerodt, Secretary of the Prussian Embassy, who spent many years in Russia
and who, unlike many foreigners, was fluent in Russian.*

(A) AN ASSESSMENT BY A BRITISH ENGINEER

Thus His Majesty, upon his return from his travels, by the example of so extensive a punishment having suppressed the enemies to his government, it was the more easy for him to go on
with those things, which he had resolved upon for the reforming
[of] his country. He began first and established not only his
Guards, which were those regiments that were fixed in the place
of the aforesaid *Streltsi,* but put his whole Army upon a new
foot, and a new discipline, which he had collected from what he
had observed abroad; and he ordered all his army to be regularly
clothed, with some distinction in the colour and trimming of the
clothes, like the custom of other nations of Europe, which had
not till now been done, but every one wore his clothes according
to his own make and fancy. He ordered also an account to be
brought to him of such persons of the nobility and gentry of considerable estates, who were not in any service or employment,
out of which he chose and commanded a great part to go and
serve as volunteers in the army, and others he ordered to attend,
and appointed them duty in several stations; some in the equipping [of] his Navy, and others he ordered to go and reside at the
frontier garrisons, that if they did no good they might be out of
the way of doing any mischief.

When he had thus disposed things in Moscow, with relation to
his Army, he went down himself to Voronezh to view those ships
and galleys that were built there by the Dutch in his absence,
and to hasten the equipment of his fleet that was preparing for
the Black Sea. He made those English that he had brought over
now his chief Master Builders, and he discharged all the Dutch
builders, except what were to finish the ships which they had be-

gun, and those who were left under the command of the English; and that there should be none but English fashion ships to be built for the future; one of which being a ship of 50 guns, His Majesty himself, immediately, as soon as he came there, set upon the stocks, a draft of which he had drawn with his own hands, and so contrived her by an invention of his own, that though the keel should be knocked off, the ship should be tight (as he proposed) which ship when he had advanced a little way, he left to be carried on by two young Russian gentlemen that had been abroad, and in company learned to build ships along with His Majesty; only he left orders for them to ask sometimes advice of the English builders when there was any occasion for it. He left also orders at Voronezh with Vice-Admiral Cruss, and Rear-Admiral Raes, together with the Sea-Captains, officers and seamen that he had taken into his service in Holland, before the time he came over to England, and who were now arrived in Voronezh, to get those ships and galleys that were built to be rigged and ready fitted to carry down to Azov, whither he intended to go with them in the spring of the year, together with his favorite Lefort, who though he knew nothing of the sea, was declared Admiral.

When His Majesty had thus settled the affairs of his Navy, as he had before done his Army, he returned back again to Moscow; where, besides what he had done at his first coming over, he made a new choice of Lords to be of his Council, and began to regulate affairs in his government, both in the Church and in the state. . . .

The Tsar also, soon after his return from his travels, gave orders to the Prikaz, or office belonging to the monasteries, that for the increase of his revenue, to ease in some measure the trading part of his people, a tax should be levied upon monasteries through all Russia, they having a great part of the best lands and villages belonging to them. As also soon after, His Majesty made an Order, that no person but what exceeded the age of 50, should be admitted into their monasteries: For the Tsar observed, that the shutting up of so many young people as they had in their monasteries, made them useless, and prevented by so much the increase of his people, which were wanting in his wars. And besides this, the Tsar had another political end in it, for he found that, by reducing their numbers, he might take part of their revenue to himself, for a less number of villages would then serve to maintain them.

It had been the manner of the Russians, like the Patriarchs of old, to wear long beards hanging down upon their bosoms, which they combed out with pride, and kept smooth and fine, without one hair to be diminished; they wore even the upper-lip of that length, that if they drank at any time, their beard dipped into the cup, so that they were obliged to wipe it when they had done, although they wore the hair of their head cut short at the same time; it being the custom only for the Popes or Priests, to wear the hair of their heads hanging down upon their backs for distinction sake. The Tsar therefore to reform this foolish custom, and to make them look like other Europeans, ordered a tax to be laid, on all gentlemen, merchants, and others of his subjects (excepting the Priests and common peasants, or slaves) that they should each of them pay 100 rubles per annum, for the wearing of their beards, and that even the common people should pay a copeck at the entrance of the gates of any of the towns or cities of Russia, where a person should be deputed at the gate to receive it as often as they had occasion to pass. This was looked upon to be little less than a sin in the Tsar, a breach of their religion, and held to be a great grievance for some time, as more particularly by being brought in by the strangers. But the women liking their husbands and sweethearts the better, they are now for the most part pretty well reconciled to this practice.

It is most certain, that the Russians had a kind of religious respect and veneration for their beards; and so much the more, because they differed herein from strangers, which was backed by the humours of the Priests, alleging that the holy men of old had worn their beards according to the model of the picture of their saints, and which nothing but the absolute authority of the Tsar, and the terror of having them (in a merry humour) pulled out by the roots, or sometimes taken so rough off, that some of the skin went with them, could ever have prevailed with the Russians to have parted with their beards. On this occasion there were letters dropped about the streets, sealed and directed to His Tsarish Majesty, which charged him with tyranny and heathenism, for forcing them to part with their beards.

About this time the Tsar came down to Voronezh, where I was then on service, and a great many of my men that had worn their beards all their lives, were now obliged to part with them, amongst which, one of the first that I met with just coming from the hands of the barber, was an old Russian carpenter that had been with me at Kamyshin, who was a very good workman with his hatchet, and whom I always had a friendship for. I jested a little with him on this occasion, telling him that he was become a young man, and asked him what he had done with his beard. Upon which he put his hand in his bosom and pulled it out and showed it to me; farther telling me, that when he came home, he would lay it up to have it put in his coffin and buried along with him, that he might be able to give an account of it to St. Nicholas, when he came to the other world; and that all his brothers (meaning his fellow-workmen who had been shaved that day) had taken the same care.

As to their clothes, the general habit which the Russians used to wear, was a long vestment hanging down to the middle of the small of their legs, and was gathered and laid in pleats upon their hips, little differing from the habit of women's petticoats.

The Tsar therefore resolving to have this habit changed, first gave orders, that all his boyars and people whatsoever, that came near his court, and that were in his pay, should, upon penalty of falling under his displeasure, according to their several abilities, equip themselves with handsome clothes made after the English fashion, and to appear with gold and silver trimming, those that could afford it. And next he commanded, that a pattern of clothes of the English fashion should be hung up at all the gates of the city of Moscow, and that publication should be made, that all persons (excepting the common peasants who brought goods and provisions into the city) should make their clothes according to the said patterns; and that whosoever should disobey the said orders, and should be found passing any of the gates of the city in their long habits, should either pay 2 grivnas (which is 20 pence) or be obliged to kneel down at the gates of the city, and to have their coats cut off just even with the ground, so much as it was longer than to touch the ground when they kneeled down, of which there were many hundreds of coats that were cut accordingly; and being done with a good humour, it occasioned mirth among the people and soon broke the custom of their wearing long coats, especially in places near Moscow, and those other towns wherever the Tsar came.

The women also, but more particularly the ladies about court, were ordered to reform the fashion of their clothes too, according to the English manner, and that which so much the more and sooner reconciled them to it, was this: It had been always the custom of Russia, at all entertainments, for the women not to be admitted into the sight or conversation with men; the very houses of all men of any quality or fashion, were built with an entrance for the women apart, and they used to be kept up separate in an apartment by themselves; only it was sometimes the custom for the master of the house, upon the arrival of any guest whom he had a mind to honour, to bring out his wife the back way from her apartment, attended with the company of her maids, to be saluted, and to present a dram of brandy round to the whole company; which being done, they used to retire back to their own apartment, and were to be seen no more. But the Tsar being not only willing to introduce the English habits, but to make them more particularly pleasing to the Russian ladies, made an order, that from thenceforward, at all weddings, and at other public entertainments, the women as well as the men, should be invited, but in an English fashioned dress; and that they should be entertained in the same room with the men, like as he had seen in foreign countries; and that the evenings should be concluded with music and dancing, at which he himself often used to be present with most of the nobility and ladies about court. And there was no wedding of any distinction, especially amongst the foreigners, but the Tsar had notice of it, and he himself would honour it with his presence, and very often gave a present to the bride, suitable to the extraordinary expense that such entertainments cost them, especially when married to the officers that were newly come into the country. At these entertainments, the Russian ladies soon reconciled themselves to the English dress, which they found rendered them more agreeable.

There was another thing also which the women very well liked in these regulations of the Tsar. It had been the custom of Russia, in case of marriages, that the match used always to be made up between the parents on each side, without any previous meeting, consent or liking of one another, though they marry very young in that country, sometimes when neither the bride nor the bridegroom are thirteen years of age, and therefore supposed not to be fit judges for themselves. The bridegroom on this occasion was not to see nor to speak to the bride but once before the day that the nuptials was to be performed; at which meeting, the friends on both sides were to come together at the bride's father's house, and then the bride was to be brought out between her maids into the room where the bridegroom was; and after a short compliment being made, she was to present the bridegroom with a dram of brandy, or other liquor, in token of her consent and good liking of his person. And afterwards all care was to be taken that she was not to see the bridegroom again until the day of marriage; and then she was to be carried with a veil all over her face, which was not to be uncovered till she came into the church. And thus this blind bargain was made.

But the Tsar taking into his consideration this unacceptable way of joining young people together without their own approbation, which might in a very great measure be reckoned to be the occasion of this discord and little love which is shewn to one another afterwards, it being a thing common in Russia to beat their wives in a most barbarous manner, very often so inhumanly that they die with the blows; and yet they do not suffer for the murder, being a thing interpreted by the law to be done by way of correction, and therefore not culpable. The wives on the other hand being thus many times made desperate, murder their husbands in revenge for the ill usage they receive; on which occasion there is a law made, that when they murder their husbands, they are set alive in the ground, standing upright, with the earth filled about them, and only their heads left just above the earth, and a watch set over them, that they shall not be relieved till they are starved to death; which is a common sight in that country, and I have known them [to] live sometimes seven or eight days in this posture. These sad prospects made the Tsar in much pity to his people, take away the occasion of these cruelties as much as possible; and the forced marriages being supposed to be one cause thereof, made an order that no young couple should be married together, without their own free liking and consent; and that all persons should be admitted to visit and see each other at least six weeks before they were married together. This new order is so well approved of, and so very pleasing to the young people, that they begin to think much better of foreigners, and to have a better liking of such other new customs as the Tsar has introduced, than they ever did before, especially amongst the more knowing and better sort of people. . . .

The Tsar, to instill principles of virtue into the minds of his people, and to give them better notions of humanity and conscience, has for 8 or 9 years past employed several persons to translate out of foreign languages, many excellent books in divinity and morality, as well as relating to war and useful arts and sciences, and has set up printing houses, and caused them to be printed in Moscow, and dispersed throughout his dominions, maugre all the opposition made thereto by the clergy; and farther, has commanded several schools of learning to be set up, and made an order, that whoever in his country that is master of an estate to the value of 500 rubles per annum, and doth not teach his son to read and write, and learn Latin, or some other foreign language, such son shall not inherit his father's estate, but the same shall be forfeited to the next heir of the same family. As also His Majesty has commanded, that the clergy of his country for the future, shall be obliged to learn Latin, or not to officiate in the priestly office. Whereby it is to be hoped, that in time his people will be brought to a better understanding in the grounds of religion and moral virtues, as well as in the art of war and trade, and other useful sciences.

His Majesty has not only done this, but takes occasion in all his private conversation to argue moderately with the chief men of the church, as well as his nobility, desiring them to be very free in satisfying him in the reasons they are able to produce for their bigotry and superstition, in adhering to their old customs. . . .

When I first went into the country the Russians dated their year from the creation of the world, which they reckoned 7206; but from whence, or what assurance they had for their account, beside the tradition of their fathers, I could never understand from them. They also reckoned the first day of their year on the first of September, which they kept with very great solemnity. The reason which they give for this beginning of their year on the first of September, and which their disputants thought to be a most convincing reason, and prided themselves in being masters of their argument, was this; That God, who was all-wise and good, created the world in the autumn, when the corn was in its full ear, and the fruits of the earth were ripe, and fit to take and eat; and not as other Europeans reckoned, in the very depth of winter, when the earth was all frozen and covered with snow. But the Tsar (sensible of their mistaken notion) desired his lords to view the map of the globe, and in a pleasant temper gave them to understand, that Russia was not all the world; that what was winter with them, was at the same time always summer in all those places beyond the equator. Besides that, according to the common way of computing the termination of the year, the seasons are considerably altered since the creation of the world, through those odd minutes that happen in every year over and above 365 days and six hours: And therefore the Tsar, to conform his country to the rest of Europe, so far as in reckoning the first day of the year on the first of January, and in dating the year with other Christians from the incarnation of our Saviour, he took the following method.

The first of January 1700, Old Style, he proclaimed a Jubilee, and commanded the same to be solemnized a whole week together, with the firing of guns, and ringing of bells; and the streets to be adorned with colours flying in the day, and illuminations at night, which all houses of any distinction were to observe; and made an order, that from that time forward, in all laws and writings whatsoever, no person, under a penalty, should date the year any longer according to the old way which the Russians had used. This he did, notwithstanding it was looked upon by the malcontents as another considerable innovation, and striking at the ground of their religion. They comply with this order out of mere fear; but there are still some of the old Russians who will get together on the first day of September, and with warm zeal still solemnize that as the first day of the new year, and privately will assert, that the world is just as old as they reckon it, which according to their account is now 7223 years. . . .

There are a great many other things which His Majesty has done to reform and convince his people of the folly of being bigoted to their old ways and customs, and that there was no real evil in changing them for new, that are either more reasonable, or more becoming and decent. The account of which would be too tedious to the reader, as well as to myself to relate. . . .

The Tsar, where he is present, does indeed give encouragement to some of those common artificers and workmen, who have the happiness to be under his eye, and whom he finds deserving, as particularly in the building and equipping of his ships, where he is daily among the artificers, and will often take the tools in hand, and work himself along with them. But his boyars are quite of another temper, and in all other places and occasions, through all the parts of the Tsar's dominions, the generality of his subjects remain still under the same check and discouragement to ingenuity: And this is certain, that if the present Tsar should happen to die, without the greatest part of his present old boyars go off before him, the generality of things wherein he has taken so much pains to reform his country, will for the most part revolve into their old form. For it is believed that his son, the present Prince of Russia, who is of a temper very much differing from his father's, and adheres to bigotry and superstition, will easily be prevailed on to come into the old methods of Russia, and quit and lay aside many of those laudable things that have been begun by the present Tsar.

Which leads me here to mention, that among some other causes, one of the chief which makes the generality of the nobility at present uneasy, is, that the Tsar obliges them against their will, to come and live at Petersburg, with their wives and their families, where they are obliged to build new houses for themselves, and where all manner of provisions are usually three or four times as dear, and forage for their horses, etc., at least six or eight times as dear as it is at Moscow, which happens from the great expense of it at Petersburg, and the small quantity which the country thereabouts produces, being more than two thirds woods and bogs; and not only the nobility, but merchants and tradesmen of all sorts, are obliged to go and live there, and to trade with such things as they are ordered, which crowd of people enhances the price of provisions, and makes a scarcity for those men who are absolutely necessary to live there, on account of the Land and Sea Service, and in carrying on those buildings and works which the Tsar has already, and farther designs to make there. Whereas in Moscow, all the lords and men of distinction, have not only very large buildings within the city, but also their country seats and villages, where they have their fish-ponds, their gardens, with plenty of several sorts of fruit and places of pleasure; but Petersburg, which lies in the Latitude of 60 degrees and 15 minutes North, is too cold to produce these things. Besides, Moscow is the native place which the Russians are fond of, and where they have their friends and acquaintances about them; their villages are near, and their provision comes easy and cheap to them, which is brought by their slaves.

As for the Tsar, he is a great lover of the water, and entirely delights in ships and boats, and in sailing, even to that degree, that in the winter, when both the River Neva, and the Head of the East Sea is frozen over, that he can no more go upon the water, then he has his boats made on purpose, and ingeniously fixed for sailing upon the ice; and every day when there is a gale of wind, unless some very extraordinary thing happen to prevent him, he sails and plies to windward upon the ice with his said boats, with Jack-Ensign and Pennant flying in the same manner as upon the water. But his lords have no relish nor pleasure in those things, and though they seemingly compliment the Tsar whenever he talks to them of the beauties and delights of Petersburg; yet when they get together by themselves, they complain and say that there are tears and water enough at Petersburg, but they pray God to send them to live again at Moscow. . . .

(B) AN ASSESSMENT BY A DUTCH DIPLOMAT

Three Men of War bought in England arrived at Riga, and another was launched at Petersburg, on which occasion the Tsar appeared in a very good humour, and discoursed with great judgment on the prosperous success of his ship-building. Among many other notable ingenious discourses which I heard held by his Tsarish Majesty on the like occurrences, there is one very remarkable, which he directed to his old Russians sitting round about him, on board that new launched Man of War, reproving them for not following the example of other Russian Ministers and Generals, and taking encouragement from their experience.

"Brethren," said he, "who is that man among you, who thirty years ago

"could have had only the thought of being employed with me in ship carpenter's work here in the Baltic; of coming hither in a German dress to settle in these countries conquered by our fatigues and bravery; of living to see so many brave and victorious soldiers and seamen sprung from Russian blood; to see our sons coming home able men from foreign countries; to see so many outlandish artificers and handicrafts men settling in our dominions, and to see the remotest Potentates express so great an esteem for us? The historians place the ancient seat of all sciences in Greece, from whence being expelled by the fatality of the times, they spread in Italy, and afterwards dispersed themselves all over Europe, but by the perverseness of our ancestors were hindered from penetrating any farther than into Poland, though the Polanders as well as the Germans formerly groped in the same darkness in which we have lived hitherto, but the indefatigable care of their governours opened their eyes at length that they made themselves masters of those arts, sciences, and improvements of life that formerly Greece boasted of. It is now our turn, if you will seriously second my designs, and add to your blind obedience a voluntary knowledge, and apply your selves to the enquiry of good and evil. I can compare this transmigration of sciences with nothing better than the circulation of the blood in the human body, and my mind almost gives me they will some time or other quit their abode in England, France, and Germany, and come to settle for some centuries among us, and perhaps afterwards return again to their original home into Greece. In the mean time I earnestly recommend to your practice the Latin saying, *Ora & labora,* pray and work, and in that case be persuaded, you may happen even in our lifetime to put other civilized nations to the blush, and to carry the glory of the Russian name to the highest pitch."

The old Russians listened with a profound silence to their haranguing Monarch, applauding him afterwards with a loud *Je je prawda* ('tis very true) and offering a ready obedience. But immediately after they fell again with great eagerness to the center of their happiness, I mean the brandy-bowl, leaving the

Tsar, who appeared very thoughtful, to study how to work about their conversion, and compass the great ends he had proposed to himself. The untowardness of these people made me astonished as well as some Russian Ministers: The many instances of their character, which I had occasion farther to observe in process of time, convinced me of the truth of the picture, which a certain French gentlemen has drawn of that nation in a letter, which for its likeness I think deserves being inserted here. "The Russians," says he,

"are the most conceited and proudest of all mankind; formerly they looked upon all other nations to be Barbarians, and fancied themselves the only polite, sensible and ingenious people in the world. Since the time that His Tsarish Majesty has perceived the ridiculousness of this conceit, and that he has forced his subjects to take instructions from foreigners, they obey, but with such inveterate pride that it hinders them from penetrating into what they are taught, and makes them upon the first tincture of knowledge fancy themselves more learned and more able than their masters, whom they hate and vex; it being impossible that presumption should yield to the obligations they owe them. What is called glory, honour, and disinterestedness, is but a chimera with them. They cannot conceive any other object of the soul but what terminates in the senses; nor can they comprehend that a foreigner of distinction who comes to serve them, should be guided by a principle different from that of getting money; hence it is that they are continually railing among themselves at foreigners, for selling their lives 'for a little money.' "

Every man will be convinced by the sequel of this journal, that though this gentleman knew the Russians perfectly well, yet he did not mention all their qualities: But the Tsar himself by his excellent judgment soon thoroughly discovered the faults of his subjects whom he used to call a herd of brutes whom he put into the shape of man, but despaired of ever breaking their obstinacy or rooting up the perverseness of their hearts. This is the reason that the travels of so many of the young Russian nobility, which they undertake well stored with money, but without any instruction or manuduction, produce no other effect than their picking out what is vicious in Germany and other countries, with a neglect of that which is good, and upon their return into Russia making such a compound of Russian vices with it as proves destructive both to the body and the soul, and will hardly ever leave room for true virtue and sincere piety in Russia. There were some Russians indeed who in their travels by their politeness and the good behaviour they had acquired, had gained the affection and esteem of some persons in Germany, who by their example were induced to believe that it was possible for a Russian to become an honest and civilized man, and consequently that the Tsar might at length be able to model his subjects into true humanity: But should one of those Germans go into Russia to search for such travellers of whom there are some thousands, and meet one or other he was formerly acquainted with, it would be hard for him to know them again after that metamorphosis which the greater part of them (I do not say all) have undergone: For they have not only thrown off again that politeness they had acquired in foreign parts, and shew an intolerable pride on account of what they may have learned there of bodily exercises (for to cultivate the mind was not their design); but also are returned again to their former way of life. However I must make this exception, that a good genius of some Russian or other, if he stays in foreign parts, may be cultivated and improved, and it can be made out by several instances that it is possible for a young Russian, by reason of that sagacity and cunning which is natural to almost the whole nation, to attain by the means of a good education and instruction abroad, to the same degree of perfection as children of other civilized nations. Those Russians of distinction, who partly are still in Germany, partly are returned home, and have distinguished themselves by their capacity, prudence and polite conduct, are instances of this assertion to the reproach of their countrymen. As for that notion which the world entertains of the Tsar's extensive knowledge, the same is entirely agreeable to truth; and there is no man who rightly knows the Tsar that can question his being the chief and most judicious Minister, the most experienced General, officer and soldier of his empire, the most learned of all Russian divines and philosophers, well versed in history and mechanics, an able shipwright, and still a better sailor; in all which sciences though he has but dull and resty disciples, yet he has put the state of war upon an admirable foot, and brought his soldiery, particularly the Infantry, to that reputation that they yield to none in the world, though they are still in great want of good officers. In short, as far as fear and blind obedience rather than wisdom of government can carry things, the Russians surpass all other nations, and should the Tsar enjoy the scepter but twenty years longer, he will do more in his dominions by this obedience than ever any other monarch did. . . .

The experience of twenty years and upwards has shewn, that notwithstanding the great expenses which the Tsar has been at in maintaining his Armies and Fleet, and carrying on so many vast buildings, yet he was not obliged to contract debts, but always found new supplies in his dominions to support his undertakings. Russia abounds in merchandise, but not in ready money, and considering the vast extent of its empire, it is justly matter of surprise, that there is such a disproportion between its extent and revenues, there being many provinces, which yield to none in the world in fruitfulness and the plentiful produce of all that is necessary for human life. The Tsar has indeed discovered [a] great part of the causes of this defect, and in some measure redressed several of them; but it is impossible for him as yet to remove the difficulties still remaining; and as for the rest, he has had neither time nor opportunity to get a true information about them. It cannot be denied that there are but few towns, and many forests and deserts in Russia, and that the greater part of the land is barren, or rather lies untilled; but one of the chief reasons of this is, that the war has deprived the country of abundance of inhabitants, and those who are left, labour under the oppression of the Tsar's officers, and of the nobility, to such a degree, that they are quite disheartened from industry, and content themselves with making a poor shift of living from hand to mouth. For in the same manner as the Tsars have exercised, time out of mind, the power of seizing the estates of their boyars, on any pretences they think sufficient; so the latter are of opinion, that, by parity of reason, they may exercise the same power over their peasants, from whence it proceeds, that all manner of industry and desire of gain is extinguished among the boors, and if by chance one happens privately to get a small sum, he hides it out of fear of his lord under a dunghill, where it lies dead to him. The nobility, on the other hand, having thus by violence and cunning drained the peasants of their very blood, and being afraid of making themselves obnoxious to the Court, by the shew of their ill-gotten wealth, commonly lock it, either up in their coffers to moulder there, or others, who are since grown wiser, convey it into the banks of London, Venice, and Amsterdam. Consequently all the money being thus concealed, both by the nobility and peasants, it has no circulation, and the country reaps no benefit from it. The Tsar was once advised to abolish slavery, and to introduce a moderate liberty, which would both encourage his subjects, and promote his own interest at the same time; but the wild temper of the Russians, who are not to be governed without constraint, was a sufficient reason for rejecting that proposition at that time.

I took great pains ever since my being in Russia, though long in vain, to get an exact calculation of the Tsar's revenues, till at length, by the assistance of some friends, I was let into the secret. I am now going faithfully to communicate to the Reader, as something unknown before, the several observations, which I partly had from the said friends, partly gathered my self at different times, and on different occasions, relating to the state of the Tsar's revenue, as it stood from 1714 to 1717, which will give an exact idea of the present state of his powerful empire. The profits accruing every year to the Tsar's treasury out of those far extended provinces, of which the Russian Empire is composed, are of three sorts, consisting either of personal service, provisions, or money. . . .

Idleness [of Moscovites] produces such numbers of beggars and rogues, and occasions so many excesses and disorders, that after sunset no body ventures abroad without sufficient company. Those villains place themselves at the corners of the streets, and throw swinging cudgels, which they call *dubines,* at the heads of those that pass by, in which practice they are so expert, that these mortal blows seldom miss. The most dangerous time is the Butter Week, when all the rabble are drunk and mad. During the last that was over before my arrival at Moscow, above sixty persons thus murdered were taken up in the streets, and I my self found two lying on the road in my journey thither. This danger on the highways increases, and consequently obliges travellers to be the more upon their guard, when the Tsar happens to be in remote parts; for then it is a common saying with those villains: *Bog vysoko; gosudar daleko;* God dwells high, and the Lord (the Tsar) is far off. It is the custom at Moscow to carry those that are found murdered in the streets out of town, and to throw them into a deep hole, and on a certain day about Whitsuntide, Priests are sent thither to say Mass for the repose of their souls, whereupon they order earth to be thrown upon them.

It is many years ago since the Tsar founded three colleges at Moscow, and provided them with several learned Russian monks, who studied in Poland, Ukrainia, and Prussia. In the first are between two and three hundred scholars, Polanders, Ukrainians, and Russians, divided into different forms, where they are taught the Principles of Literature by monks, who are able men, and of good sense. They shewed me their buildings and churches, and gave me an account of their method of teaching; and afterwards a student of the first form, who was a young *kniaz*, made a handsome speech in Latin, for which he had prepared himself, and which consisted of compliments. The second college is for all the Mathematical Sciences, in which are near seven hundred scholars, who, according to their capacity, are ranged in three forms, and are kept under a strict discipline. The Masters are Russians, and their Head an Englishman, thoroughly versed in the Russian tongue, who has already sent many youths well instructed both to the Sea and Land Service. At my being there he sent, pursuant to the Tsar's orders, one hundred more to the new erected Academy of the Marine at Petersburg, after having given them the first tincture by his instructions, and he himself has since been sent for thither to be Professor in the said Academy. The boys in the third college are only taught Navigation, and what belongs to it. . . .

My coming into the church [to observe the consecration of a Nun] occasioned no small surprise among the female congregation there, who knew nothing of my having leave for it from the Abbess and the Archbishop; the curiosity of some of the ladies was such, that they began to pull me by the sleeve, and to enter into conversation with me. They not only asked me, what country I was of, what business I had at Moscow, and the like, they even enquired whether I was baptized, and a Christian, because I did not bow, and fall to the ground as they did; which I excused, by saying, that this was an outward ceremony, which was not customary with us. However, this conversation made room for another after the solemnity was over, when they detained me with great civility near an hour, asking many questions relating to Germany; particularly about the ladies there, and whether they were kept so close and low as they are in Russia. They seemed greatly pleased with the account I gave them, and on our parting gave me to understand, that they should be glad to be married in that country. I have observed above, that the Russian wives and daughters are kept extremely retired, and never go abroad, unless it be to church, or to see their nearest relations. I have seen many a beautiful face among them, but they are disgraced by their old customs, which they cannot yet leave off, the court being too far off to break them of them. Ladies of quality are dressed after the German fashion, which indeed they prefer to their old antique dress; but as to their courtesies, still the old custom prevails of bowing with the head to the ground. There are those ladies, who have made some stay with their husbands in foreign countries, but, upon their return to Moscow, are obliged to throw off foreign manners, and conform with the old way, for fear of being laughed out of countenance by their former acquaintance; but at Petersburg they have the Tsar's rigorous orders on their side. All the comfort the old-fashioned ladies have in this spreading reformation of manners, is now and then to remember with pleasure, the good old time when the Court ladies attended a Tsarina's coach on horse-back in Amazons dress. If a Russian gives an entertainment to persons not related to him, the mistress of the house does either not appear at all, or only just before dinner, to make the guests welcome with a kiss and a cup of brandy, after which she makes her *poklon* or courtesy, and gets out of the way again. Five years ago there was a project on foot, for sending the youngest and handsomest Russian ladies to travel abroad, as well as their brothers, at the expense of their parents, to Königsberg, Berlin, Dresden, and other places, to board in families, in order to learn foreign customs and languages, and all sort of female work. But upon the remonstrances of the parents, that the freedom of foreign conversation would expose their children to great temptations, and endanger their virtue and reputation, this design was dropped. He

that endeavours to oblige a fine woman by a compliment, calls
her *krasnaia devitsa,* or red maid[1]; for they think, the more red,
the greater beauty; hence it is, that the sex paint to excess in this
country, and those of a middling rank put abundance of patches
on their daubed faces, which extravagance was carried so far not
long ago, that they wore patches of variety of figures, even trees,
coaches and horses, and the like. The women in general, the
quality excepted, still wear furs under their coats, even in summer time; those who frequent the court, appear indeed perfectly
well dressed after the foreign fashion; but in conversation with
strangers, they cannot yet conquer their in-born bashfulness and
awkwardness. As for what concerns the common tradition, that
the Russian women judge of the love of their husbands by the
blows they receive from them, the same ought to be taken in a
right sense. They are indeed very ill used, and kept under a severe discipline; but who would imagine them to be fond of being
beaten? The truth is, they are so given to drinking, and other ill
habits, (I speak of the common sort) that they neglect their
household affairs, whence it happens, that the man, if he has the
education of his children and other domestic concerns at heart,
either provoked by the carelessness of his wife, or even sometimes
prompted by his own ill humour, lashes her as long as he thinks
that rude way of correction may reclaim her, or at least till his
mad fits are over. But if he finds her past hopes, or falls into ill
courses himself, he begins to leave his wife and children to themselves, and to follow other women. In this case it is natural for a
woman to infer from her husband's beating her no more, that he
has withdrawn his affection, and abandoned himself to forbidden pleasures. . . .

At those assemblies [social gatherings in Petersburg] there is
dancing in one room, in another people are playing at cards,
draughts, but particularly at chess, in which even the meanest
Russians excel; in a third room there is a company smoking and
discoursing together, and in the fourth are ladies and gentlemen
diverting themselves with questions and commands, forfeits,
cross-purposes, and other such little plays, that create good humour and laughter. Though none of the company are obliged to

[1] *Krasnaia devitsa* actually means beautiful maid. Ed.

drink any more wine or brandy than what they ask for, except one transgresses the established rules or laws of the assembly, which happens very often, yet there are many good Russians, who lay hold of that opportunity of making much of themselves at other men's cost, and look upon assemblies as one of the most laudable innovations that have been introduced in their native country. It falls to the turn of every great man of the Court to keep an assembly once in a winter at least; and if the Tsar pitches upon a particular person for it, notice is given to him by the Master of the Police.

Operas and plays will also be in fashion in process of time, and they are now looking out for a fund for those diversions, though the Tsar himself has as little inclinations that way as he has for hunting, or the like. His subjects indeed have made some attempts for acting on the Stage, but with very indifferent success, for want of proper rules. The Princess Natalia once had the direction of a tragedy, which was represented before the Tsar's last travels, and at which every body was admitted. She had caused a large empty house to be fitted up, and to be divided into pit and boxes. The actors and actresses were ten in number, all native Russians, who had never been abroad, so that it is easy to judge of their ability. The tragedy it self, as well as the farce, were in Russian, and of the Princess's own composition, being a compound of sacred and profane history. I was told, that the subject related to one of the late rebellions in Russia, represented under disguised names. The piece was interspersed with the drolleries of a Harlequin, who was an officer of the Army, and ended with an Epilogue, setting forth the contents of the tragedy, and concluding with a Moral reflecting on the horrors of rebellion, and the unhappy events it commonly issues in. The orchestra was composed of sixteen musicians, all Russians, whose performances was suitable to that of the rest. They are taught music, as well as other sciences, by the help of the *batogs,* without which discipline nothing goes down with them, as I have been told by diverse officers, and is confirmed by daily experience. If a General pitches upon some spare fellow in a regiment, whom he will have to learn music, notwithstanding he has not the least notion of it, nor any talent that way, he is put out to a Master, who gives him a certain time for learning his task; as, first, the handling of the instrument, then to play some Lutheran hymn, which are their airs, or some minuet, and so on; if the scholar has not learnt his lesson during the term prefixed, the *batogs* are applied, and repeated till such time as he is master of the tune. The same method is made use of in all other things, particularly in military exercises. This severe discipline produces such a blind obedience among these people towards their superiors, as appears particularly among the soldiers, who shew themselves faithful and indefatigable in the service, and, notwithstanding their gross ignorance, learn to practice what is required of a good soldier.

I will conclude this discourse concerning the intended embellishing of Petersburg, with what I once heard the Prince Menshikov say, *viz.* that Petersburg should become another Venice, to see which foreigners would travel thither purely out of curiosity. Setting aside the perpetual objection of the raw climate of the place, it is possible his saying might prove true in time, if the Russians would be less refractory to the Tsar's intentions, and use strangers better than they do at present, as likewise if passengers were allowed more liberty than hitherto, in going thither, and returning from thence, and if care was taken to provide against the excessive dearness of all necessaries of life at Petersburg.

(C) AN ASSESSMENT BY A PRUSSIAN DIPLOMAT

During his reign Peter I made not even the slightest change in the realm of faith, and especially in the dogma of the Church; on the contrary, he always expressed a real desire to preserve the purity of religious teachings, and he tried to force back [into the Orthodox faith] the so-called dissenters or schismatics, who had broken away from the Church during the reign of his father, by imposing on them an extraordinary tax, an unusual corvée, the wearing of degrading clothing, and other similar humiliating oppressive measures. He even ordered the burning at the stake of some of their leaders.

It is true that during his time in the teaching about the communion they began to use in Russia the word "transubstantiation" instead of "transmutation," which the Russian Church had used up to that time. In a Catechism published at his order, one can also find some modifications in the teaching about the icons. . . .

But in the hierarchy, and in the ceremony of the Russian Church, Peter I conceived various fundamental changes, and by-and-large brought these to a successful conclusion. The most important change that served as a starting point for all other changes was the abolishment of the Patriarchate in Moscow, and Peter I's appointment of himself as the supreme bishop, or the head of his Church. . . .

Among the changes which Peter I introduced in the ceremony of the Church, one should also include the permission and the legalization of marriages between foreigners of other faiths and Russian women, which hitherto had been prohibited, and which the new Synod approved. Under the new rules, such marriages became legal on condition: 1) that the foreigner first declare himself a subject of the Russian state and pledge to serve it until death; 2) that the children of both sexes be christened and brought up in the Russian faith; and 3) that the foreigner would try neither by force nor persuasion to change the faith of his wife, and to that end he would always allow free entry into his house to an [Orthodox] priest assigned to supervise it. . . .

The discovery [of administrative corruption and inefficiency] forced Peter I to take two steps. First, he developed a taste for investigation, which he preserved [to the end of his life], and which corresponded with his natural inclination for sternness; second, Peter I expressed a desire to introduce in the internal administration of his country, similarly as he adopted for the military, the same kind of order that prevailed in other European countries. Having acknowledged the Swedes as his teachers in military affairs, he thought that their administrative and financial institutions could also be introduced in his state with the same success. He became so obsessed with this idea that, without consulting anyone, in 1716 he secretly sent to Sweden a person, giving him plenty of money to secure the rules and regulations of Swedish Colleges. He liked these so much that, without any further investigation as to whether these institutions were applicable to Russian conditions or not, and to what extent, he immediately decided to introduce them in Russia. Toward that end he hired a multitude of Germans to serve as Vice Presidents, Councillors, and Secretaries of these Colleges. Early in 1719, these institutions were opened in Petersburg. But it was soon discovered that all this had been done in too great a hurry, and that in administration it would cause more confusion than the anticipated order of precision. . . . The confusion was caused by the inability of the old Russian officials to adapt themselves [to the new institutions]. Though they may have had an understanding of their country, Russian Councillors in Colleges were unable to grasp clearly the meaning [and operation] of the new order. The Germans seldom could understand the problem, first because they did not know the Russian language, and, second, because very few among them knew anything about Swedish institutions.

In 1722 this situation forced Peter I to change his new Colleges for the second time. He dismissed the majority of foreigners, and, except for retaining their German names, the Colleges were reorganized in such a way that they resembled closely the old Russian order. The only thing that differentiated them [from the old prikazes] was a multitude of officials. . . .

Among all of his innovations, Peter I worked on no other project more zealously and with greater dedication and patience than on the building of his Navy. In all other areas he limited himself to the inspection of the main plan and left the execution of details to those he appointed to be in charge. But when the matter was connected with the Navy he inspected every minute detail. Nothing happened in the Admiralty, not even one nail was nailed down, without first reporting it to him, and without getting his approval to do it. Not one day passed by without his being in the Admiralty to watch the construction of ships for several hours, and if he found something to do there he set aside everything else. No victory brought him as much satisfaction as any insignificant advantage that his ships or galleys may have gained [over the enemy]. He celebrated jubilantly the capture of one bad frigate and six old galleys as if it were a great triumph— which obviously it was not. When his galleys captured four small Swedish vessels at Grengham, to commemorate that event he ordered the construction of a huge victory memorial in the front of the Senate Building in Petersburg. Correspondingly, nothing embittered him more than some insignificant accident involving his ships. Then only God could help a person who could be said to have been in some way responsible for that accident! . . . .

From the very beginning [of his reign] he intended to give a satisfactory education to his nobles by sending them abroad, similarly as he himself had learned by observing in European countries. As soon as he returned from his first major trip, he dispatched to England, Holland, France, and Italy, a sufficiently large number of coarse and uneducated young people he selected from among the most distinguished families of the country. But, since they brought back just slightly more knowledge than they took with them, he came to the conclusion that they were deficient in basic knowledge, and he decided to eliminate that deficiency by introducing indispensable schools, and the Academy. . . .

[Following Russian conquest of Marienburg] Peter became acquainted with a [Swedish] pastor named Glück, whom he consulted about introducing some schools. This man had as much education as one can normally expect of a Swedish village pastor. But because he knew Russian, Peter I considered him a beacon of the enlightened world. Yet, his outlook was so narrow that he failed to provide Peter I with anything worthwhile, except to suggest that he introduce the same kind of schools that existed in Livonia, where children could study the Catechism, Latin, and other school subjects. Peter I approved this advice, asked the pastor to carry it out, and gave him the necessary funds and a large home in Moscow. The pastor then selected students from a Lutheran Seminary and organized his school in exact conformity with the rules of the Swedish Church Statute. To prevent the development of any shortcomings, he made a poor translation of Lutheran songs into Russian. The children were to sing these songs solemnly before and after lessons.

The sad part of this institution and the deplorable outcome of such teaching of Russian youth were obvious immediately, with the result that [everyone knew that] these schools could not last long. Peter I soon ordered them closed, and decreed that parents provide their children with elementary education either with the aid of private tutors, or in Lutheran schools in Moscow, or through local Catholic priests. Meanwhile, he concentrated his efforts exclusively on the problem of how to make his nobles knowledgeable in engineering and navigation matters, and for that purpose he opened in Moscow and Petersburg various academies where the Russian youth could study these sciences as well as mathematics.

For a time this remained his prime concern in the area of science. If he did anything to advance science, it was mostly in physical and medical spheres, where he found special satisfaction.

But when, in 1717, the French Academy of Sciences accepted him as a member, this created in him a strong desire to organize a similar Academy in his empire. His own views on science were somewhat nebulous to enable him to decide what was useful for his country and what was not. His views became even more confusing, thanks to the advice he received on that subject from various scholars unfamiliar with Russia's natural conditions. Finally, in 1724, he decided to make the French Academy the example for his and, to give it luster at the beginning, he attracted several scholars with reputation; namely, [Christian] Wolff, [Jacob] Hermann, [Joseph] Delisle, and [Nicholas] Bernoulli. He assigned the customs houses of Narva, Dorpat,, and Pernov to provide funds for the [Academy's] expenditures, which reached 25,000 rubles annually. Since he died shortly after this, he had no satisfaction of seeing this institution in operation. His court physician, Blumenrost, who acted as Chairman [of the Academy] with 3,000 rubles annual salary, thanks to the trust the Empress [Catherine I] had in him, prepared everything properly and Catherine approved the Academy. He [Blumenrost] was also able to secure steady support from Peter II [1727–1730], in spite of that fact that the majority of Senators considered it a useless and poorly conceived institution that brought no benefits to the country, and were eager to terminate financial support for it.

The change in clothing and style [by Peter I] was introduced only for nobles, officials, and the townspeople. Priests and peasants retained the right to preserve their beards and to wear the old style of clothing. To date [1736-7], the beard remains an essential external part of priestly appearance. The change of clothing gave Peter I little or no trouble. Everyone submitted willingly to his wish and objected only to the style. They argued that the German frock-coat, especially in such a cold climate [as that in Russia], did not provide as adequate a warmth as did Russian [clothing], although it required the same amount of material.

But the beard found a multitude of ardent spokesmen, especially among the common people, who suddenly perceived that if they should part with this ornament God's image would be destroyed. Consequently, many among them preferred placing their heads under the axe to parting with the beard. Although the [Holy] Synod made public a special statement, wherein it tried to prove in great detail that the beard in no way reflected God's image, there still were among the townspeople many who did not believe in the accuracy of these assurances, and who preferred all sufferings to subjecting their beards to the razor. This forced the government to place a tax on the right to wear a beard, and they willingly and eagerly pay it annually.

The rest of the people became so completely detached from the style of their previous clothing and their beards that if they were to be given an opportunity of restoring their earlier freedoms and the old form of government, it is certain that they would not return to their previous style of clothing.

This can be said about [the change of] their customs with certainty: there was, for example, an old custom in Russia that during the marriage ceremony the bride covered her face. In the middle of the ceremony she was led from the ceremonial table to a bed, and then they brought to the table the evidence of her virginity. Now all influencial people, including merchants and townspeople, find this and similar strange customs at weddings and other observances quite ridiculous and indecent. Today such customs are observed only in provinces by the common people.

Then it is likewise difficult to suppose that women, who, according to an ancient Russian custom, were required to lead very isolated lives and were not allowed to speak with anyone, would now abandon the freedom they gained during Peter I's reign, even though they are still today far behind [the rights women enjoy in] France, Poland, or, for that matter, Germany . . .

Finally, important people of both sexes, including many townspeople, have adopted from their contacts with foreigners a great deal of politeness and the more proper rules of conduct and of social behavior that prevail in Europe. But they do not follow them. It is quite shocking to see how some of the foremost people grossly violate these rules. Thus, in such spheres of activity as eating, drinking, home decorating, and the like, today's Russian remains an old Russian. No matter how long a young Russian nobleman may live abroad and adopt a very polite and courteous appearance, the moment he returns home and rejoins his family he reverts back to the old style of life, and those who may have seen him somewhere else a year before will not recognize him.

But the Russians are able least of all to cast off their irresistible aversion to those rules which Peter I introduced in the state administration. They ardently desire to free themsleves from the punishing whip of foreigners, and they wish to re-establish the old form of administration. The memory of Peter I is respected only by the common people, by people of the lower ranks, and by soldiers, especially guardsmen, who cannot forget the significance and the distinction they received during his reign. The rest, even though they heap on him beautiful praises in public, when one gets the opportunity to know them and to get their trust, sing an entirely different song. . . . They attribute to him the most slanderous debauchery and the most horrible cruelties that are very difficult to believe. They even maintain that he was not the real son of Tsar Aleksei, but the son of a German doctor who was secretly substituted by Tsarina Natalia in place of a daughter she had given birth to. They can tell many details about it. Consequently, they attribute to that not only his inclination toward foreign habits and customs, but also such of his various medical operations as the extration of teeth, and the like. They also point out that he was ashamed of noble surroundings, and behaved no better with nobles than with common craftsmen. Finally, they mention as proof [for their beliefs] his unwillingness to have a Russian or a foreign princess as his wife; instead, they say, he selected as his wife a common peasant girl from Livonia, who, before reaching him, had previously passed through other hands. About his bravery and other attributes that are ascribed to him, they also have a different view than that which has been formulated abroad. Most of the time they give very strange and not very flattering reasons. They laugh at his innovative rules and institutions. They consider Petersburg and the Navy as abominations, and supply ample evidence to prove their contentions.

They even consider useless and harmful the establishment of the standing Army, which the rest of the world believes was the greatest achievement of Peter I for his empire. They are firmly convinced that if they would not interfere in other people's quarrels without any good cause, none of their neighbors would attack them, and that, at any rate, their old military forces were sufficient to repel the enemy from their frontiers. They also consider the new Army dangerous, because they believe that a properly trained Army, bound by new ties that are fully subordinate to the autocratic whim of the sovereign, should he happen to be unjust or eccentric, would deprive them of peace and leisure which they could enjoy at home; instead, they will be forced to serve in the Army, which in their view is a great burden; they also consider those who serve voluntarily as great ignoramuses. . . .

3 An Assessment of Peter I's Changes by an Eighteenth-Century Russian Historian-Prince

Among his own subjects Peter I's modernization efforts encountered many supporters, as well as critics. The most articulate spokesman for the critics in the eighteenth century was Prince Michael M. Shcherbatov (1733–1790). Prince Shcherbatov, a descendant of an ancient Russian aristocratic family, was one of the most cultured Russians of his time. An ardent follower of Voltaire, he believed in the progress and modernization that Peter I had achieved for Russia. He was critical, however, of the price that Russian people, and especially the aristocrats, had to pay for that modernization. Shcherbatov wrote the following assessment of Peter I's reign sometime around 1787, but it was not published until 1896.

SOURCE. Prince M. M. Shcherbatov, *On the Corruption of Morals in Russia.* Edited and Translated with an Introduction and Notes by A. Lentin (Cambridge, England: Cambridge University Press, 1969), pp. 135–157 (alternate pages). Reprinted by permission of Cambridge University Press.

Peter the Great, in imitating foreign nations, not only strove to introduce to his realm a knowledge of sciences, arts and crafts, a proper military system, trade, and the most suitable forms of legislation; he also tried to introduce the kind of sociability, social intercourse and magnificence, which he first learnt from Lefort, and which he later saw for himself. Amid essential legislative measures, the organization of troops and artillery, he paid no less attention to modifying the old customs which seemed crude to him. He ordered beards to be shaved off, he abolished the old Russian garments, and instead of long robes he compelled the men to wear German coats, and the women, instead of the 'telogreya' to wear bodices, skirts, gowns and 'samaras', and instead of skull-caps, to adorn their heads with fontanges and cornettes. He established various assemblies where the women, hitherto segregated from the company of men, were present with them at entertainments.

It was pleasant for the female sex, who had hitherto been almost slaves in their own homes, to enjoy all the pleasures of society, to adorn themselves with clothes and fineries, which enhanced the beauty of their faces and set off their fine figures. It also gave them no small pleasure to be able to see in advance with whom they were to be joined for life, and that the faces of their husbands and betrothed were no longer covered with prickly beards.

And on the other hand, it was pleasant for men who were young and not set in the old ways to mix freely with the female sex and to be able to see in advance and make the acquaintance of their brides-to-be; for previously they married, relying on their parents' choice.

The passion of love, hitherto almost unknown in an age of crude customs, began to overwhelm sensitive hearts, a change that first made itself felt through the action of the senses. And this in itself meant that women, previously unaware of their beauty, began to realize its power; they began to try to enhance it with suitable clothes, and used far more luxury in their adornments than their ancestors. Oh, how the desire to be pleasing acts upon women's senses! I have heard on good authority that there was then only one ladies' hairdresser in Moscow, and that whenever the young women had to have their hair dressed for some festival, she would prepare some of them three days in advance, and these were obliged to sleep sitting up until the day of the party so as not to spoil their head-dress. Perhaps this will not be believed today, but I repeat that I heard it on such good authority, that there should be no doubt about it.

If the passion to be pleasing produced such an effect on women, it could not fail to have an effect on men too, who wished to be attractive to them; thus, the same striving after adornment gave rise to the same luxury. And now they ceased to be content with one or two long coats, but began to have many made, with galoon, embroidery and point-d'espagne.

The monarch himself kept to the old simplicity of morals in his dress, so that apart from plain coats and uniforms, he never wore anything costly; and it was only for the coronation of the Empress Catherine Alexeevna, his wife, that he had made a coat of blue gros-de-tours with silver-braid; they say he also had another coat, grey with gold braid, but I do not know for what great occasion this was made.

The rest was all so plain that even the poorest person would not wear it today, as can be seen from such of his clothes as have remained, and are kept in the Kunst-Kamera at the Imperial Academy of Sciences.

He disliked cuffs and did not wear them, as his portraits attest. He had no costly carriages, but usually travelled in a gig in towns, and in a chaise on a long journey.

He did not have a large number of retainers and attendants, but had orderlies, and did not even have a bodyguard, apart from a Colonel of the Guard.

However, for all his personal simplicity, he wanted his subjects to have a certain magnificence. I think that this great monarch, who did nothing without farsightedness, had it as his object to stimulate trade, industries and crafts through the magnificence and luxury of his subjects, being certain that in his lifetime excessive magnificence and voluptuousness would not enthrone themselves at the royal court.

And so we find that he encouraged a certain magnificence in dress; we see that during the triumphal entry, after the capture of

Azov, Admiral-of-the-Fleet Lefort wore a red coat with galoon along the seams, and the other Commanders also wore rich coats; for in those days Commanders did not wear uniform.

Wealthy court dignitaries, and men who had been enriched by his benefactions, such as the Trubetskoys, Sheremetev and Menshikov, now strove to have rich clothes on ceremonial occasions. Brocade and galoon came into fashion for men and women alike, and although such clothes were not often worn, and although fashions lasted a long time, nevertheless they now existed, and according to their means, people now had them made more often than in the time of the old customs.

Instead of sledges and horseback-riding, and instead of the 'kolymagas', which were impossible to decorate, carriages and coaches now appeared; the coach-and-six, hitherto unknown, now came into existence, together with decorations suitable for these vehicles. Servants now dressed in the German fashion; they no longer arrayed themselves in multi-coloured garments, but each master made liveries for them, according to his coat-of-arms or his private whim; but stewards, of whom there were still very few, still dressed in multi-coloured garments.

As far as his domestic life was concerned, although the monarch himself was content with the plainest food, he now introduced drinks previously unknown in Russia, which he drank in preference to other drinks; namely, instead of domestic brandy, brewed from ordinary wine—Dutch aniseed brandy which was called 'state' brandy, and Hermitage and Hungarian wine, previously unknown in Russia.

His example was followed by the grandees and those who were close to the court; and indeed it was proper for them to provide these wines; for the monarch was fond of visiting his subjects, and what should a subject not do for the monarch?

True, this was far from being to his liking; on the contrary, he was often angered by it, and would drink not only a sweetened brandy made of ordinary wine, but even the ordinary wine itself. But their own desire for a pleasure hitherto unknown to them prevailed even over the monarch's order forbidding the imitation of his taste. Houses were now stocked not only with the 'state' aniseed brandy, but also with Danzig brandies; not only with the traditional wines which I mentioned above, but also with Hermitage, Hungarian wine, and several others.

True, in the beginning they were still served very sparingly, and in average households they were never used at ordinary meals, but only at festivals and feasts; and even here they were not ashamed to bring in a sealed quart or flagon, and having poured a glassful from it for each guest, to seal it up again and send it back to the cellar.

Peter the Great did not like feasts himself, and had no time to hold them at his court. He therefore left this to his favourite, Prince Menshikov, who held them often, both on ceremonial occasions and for Ministers from abroad, with great magnificence for that time. For this he had a house that was large, not only for those days, but even for today (for the Land Cadet Corps was later accommodated in it), and I have heard that often the monarch, looking from his palace and seeing feasting and celebrations in his favourite's house, was pleased, and would say: 'See how Danilych makes merry!'

Closely copying him, as they were bound to do by their very rank, other leading officials of the Empire also kept open table, such as Admiral-of-the-Fleet, Count Fyodor Matveevich Apraxin, Field-Marshal-in-Chief, Count Boris Petrovich Sheremetev, the Chancellor, Count Gavrilo Ivanovich Golovkin, and the boyar, Tikhon Nikitich Streshnev, who as first ruler of the Empire during Peter the Great's absence abroad, was given estates in order to provide for such meals.

As these eminent men were copied by their inferiors, so the custom of keeping an open table was now introduced in many homes. The meals were not of the traditional kind, that is, when only household products were used; now they tried to improve the flavour of the meat and fish with foreign seasonings. And of course, in a nation in which hospitality has always been a characteristic virtue, it was not hard for the custom of these open tables to become a habit; uniting as it did the special pleasure of society and the improved flavour of the food as compared with the traditional kind, it established itself as a pleasure in its own right.

Peter the Great was no enemy to polite society; but he wanted it to be inexpensive for all. He established the Assemblies, at which large numbers gathered on special days. But for these Assemblies he prescribed rules on printed sheets, concerning what should be served at table and how guests were to be received, thereby averting both excessive luxury and the burden of entertaining the higher orders. For sociability does not consist in overeating and drinking, and it cannot be agreeable where there is no equality. The monarch himself was often present at these Assemblies, and kept a strict watch that his orders were carried out.

But these barriers were weak—whenever taste, man's natural voluptuousness and luxury strove to break down the barrier placed in their way, and whenever inequality of rank and the hope of receiving something from the grandees destroyed equality. In the monarch's presence, the orders he had laid down were obeyed at the Assemblies, but in private life, luxury and abasement took root.

And indeed, we see that many noble houses had already begun to decline by then, and as they declined they began to expect support from the monarch's favour and the grandees' protection.

Among the first of the great houses to fall I have heard of that of Prince Ivan Vasil'evich Odoevsky, whose house was on the Tverskaya in the parish of the Saviour (the same house which after his death belonged to Vasily Fyodorovich Saltykov, then to Stroganov, and now belongs to Prince Alexei Borisovich Golitsyn). This Prince Odoevsky so ruined himself by his immoderate voluptuousness, that, having sold all his estates, he only left himself with a small number of servants. These were musicians, and by going round to various places to play, and receiving payment, they thereby kept him for the rest of his life. Truly, under the old simplicity of morals, musicians would not have found sufficient profit in their art to keep both themselves and their master.

I spoke of this Prince Odoevsky, as of a man who ruined himself, but there were many others too, who, if not brought to ruin by this transformation in our way of life, at any rate experienced no little hardship. To mention no others, Boris Petrovich Sheremetev, the Field Marshal, renowned for his deeds, though enriched by the monarch's favour, was obliged to take his state salary in advance, and died in debt on this account, as his actual will attests. And after his death his wife petitioned the monarch that, as a result of law-suits and other losses, she had been brought to ruin.

With this change in the way of life, first of the leading officials of state, and then, by imitation, of the other nobles, and as expenditure reached such a point that it began to exceed income, people began to attach themselves more and more to the monarch and to the grandees, as sources of riches and rewards.

I fear someone may say that this, at any rate, was a good thing, that people began to attach themselves more and more to the monarch. No, this attachment was no blessing, for it was not so much directed to the person of the monarch as to personal ends; this attachment became not the attachment of true subjects who love their sovereign and his honour and consider everything from the point of view of the national interest, but the attachment of slaves and hirelings, who sacrifice everything for their own profit and deceive their sovereign with obsequious zeal.

Courseness of morals decreased, but the place left by it was filled by flattery and selfishness. Hence came sycophancy, contempt for truth, beguiling of the monarch, and the other evils which reign at court to this day and which have ensconced themselves in the houses of the grandees.

This vice did not escape the notice of the sharp-witted monarch; stern and just in the extreme, he tried to eliminate flattery as much as possible. It happened, as I have heard, that a certain officer known to him, being with him at an Assembly, boasted of his zeal for the monarch, saying that he was ready to die for him in any circumstances.

Hearing this, the monarch told him that he did not wish, nor did his duty dictate, that he should want to die for him irrespective of circumstances; it simply asked that, in case of necessity or danger to his person, which was closely linked to the national interest, he should be prepared to sacrifice his life. The officer, wishing to make further show of his zeal, began to reaffirm that he was ready to do so at any hour the monarch pleased. The sharp-witted monarch, making no reply, took his hand, placed his finger against a burning candle, and began to scorch it. The officer, in pain, began to try and pull back his hand. Then, releasing it, the monarch said to him: if he could not endure the small pain of having his finger scorched, not by necessity but at the monarch's will, how could he so generously promise that he would gladly sacrifice his whole body without need?

Another instance which I have heard proves how much the monarch loved the truth. Zakhar Danilych Mishukov, a Lieutenant in the Fleet before 1718, was a favourite of the monarch, being the first Russian in whom he had found an adequate knowledge of navigation, and the first Russian who already commanded a frigate. Being at a feast at Kronstadt together with the monarch, and becoming rather drunk, he began to reflect on the monarch's age, on his apparently weak health, and on the heir he was leaving. Suddenly he burst into tears.

The monarch, who was sitting next to him, was astonished at his flowing tears, and, curious, asked the reason for them. Mishukov replied: he had been reflecting that the place where they were sitting, the capital city built nearby, the new fleet, the many Russians who were becoming sailors, he himself, who served in the fleet and was conscious of his favour—all this was the work of his hands; when he considered this and noticed that the health of his sovereign and benefactor was weakening, he could not refrain from tears, adding quite candidly: 'To whom will you leave us?' The monarch replied: 'I have an heir', meaning the Czarevich Alexei Petrovich. Whereupon Mishukov, blindly and carelessly said: 'Oh! but he's stupid, he'll undo everything!'

To speak thus before the monarch about his heir, and that not in secret, but before a large assembly! But what did the monarch do? He immediately realized not only the boldness and coarseness but also the truth of the remark, and laughing, was content to hit him on the head, adding: 'Fool! this is not to be said in company.'

But despite such a love of truth and his aversion to flattery, the monarch could not eradicate this encroaching venom. Most of those around him did not dare to contradict him in anything, but rather flattered him, praising everything he did, and never resisting his whims, while some even indulged his passions.

Although he was never blatantly deceived, yet Prince Yakov Fyodorovich Dolgoruky, in his opposition to the monarch in the Senate, never found any supporters. And in vain with his stern and just observations did he cause two ordinances, signed by the monarch, to be cancelled: (concerning the transport by post-horses of provisions for the army at St Petersburg, and concerning the recruitment of forced labour at public expense, for the construction of the Ladoga Canal). Neither in these two cases, nor in any others, would anyone become a partner to his resoluteness and justice. Only the monarch himself endured his rough but just observations, and overcoming his indignation, would agree with them, albeit reluctantly.

I have heard from eye-witnesses, and Vasily Nikitich Tatishchev has included this in his History, that when the monarch was at a feast in Kronstadt, the grandees around him began to laud him with praises, saying that he was greater than his father. Amid such paeans of praise, Prince Yakov Fyodorovich Dolgoruky alone remained silent. Noticing this, the monarch asked his opinion.

This shrewd and resolute man could not reply immediately to such a question, involving a judgement between the reigning monarch and his father, both distinguished for their qualities. After some moments' thought, he spoke as follows: he recounted in detail all that Peter the Great had done for the good of the country, he recounted his labours and feats, and finally, said how great he was among earthly rulers; but, continuing, he said: 'All these labours, all these measures, still do not ensure the inner peace of the realm and the security of the life and property of the citizens. Your father (he said) began much at a time of tranquillity of morals, but of all he did the greatest is the Code of Laws, which, now that customs have changed, also needs to be changed. When you have crowned all your feats with good laws, then it will be possible to say with justice that you have by far surpassed your father.' The monarch felt the full justice of his words and confirmed his opinion with his own assent.

Why was it that no one else, whether in conversation, in the Senate, or anywhere, spoke such truth as this Prince Dolgoruky, a man worthy of immortality? It was because they were more anxious to obtain the monarch's favour, than, by speaking the truth, to obtain his respect; they wanted rank and property.

For indeed, his favourite, Prince Menshikov, does not seem ever to have stated the strict truth to him; Gavrilo Ivanovich Golovkin, the State Chancellor, does not seem to have discouraged him from his correspondence with Gyllenborg, Görtz, and the English and Scots accomplices of the Pretender; (but it was Ostermann who was then of low rank and had written the necessary letter, who pointed out the impropriety of this policy;) Ivan Musin-Pushkin does not seem to have restrained him from any action; Admiral Apraxin, who enjoyed such confidence, does not seem to have contradicted the monarch in anything. They all merely expressed their agreement, and for their own profit allowed flattery and servility to take root, against which the monarch himself and Prince Yakov Fyodorovich Dolgoruky were striving.

And on the other hand, the ecclesiastics, who disliked him for taking away their power, sang forth his praises in church. Among these was Prokopovich, a churchman, who, though he had no dislike for the monarch, was completely blinded by ambition, as he clearly showed in other reigns. He raised his grandiloquent voice in the monarch's praises. The monarch was worthy of much praise; but it is to be wished that it had not proceeded from flattery; but the praises of Prokopovich, that unshorn friar, that ambitious prelate, who sacrified religion to the whims of Bühren (for though an archbishop of the Church of God, he was not ashamed to be a judge in the Secret Chancellory) ;—his praises were those of a flatterer, as is attested by his own book *The Truth of the Monarch's Will,* a monument of flattery and monkish fawning before the monarch's whim.

I said that it was voluptuousness and luxury that were able to produce such an effect in men's hearts; but there were also other causes, stemming from actual institutions, which eradicated resoluteness and good behavior.

The abolition of rights of precedence (a custom admittedly harmful to the service and the state), and the failure to replace it by any granting of rights to the noble families, extinguished thoughts of noble pride in the nobility. For it was no longer birth that was respected, but ranks and promotions and length of service. And so everyone started to strive after ranks; but since not everyone is able to perform straightforward deeds of merit, so for lack of meritorious service men began to try and worm their way up, by flattering and humouring the monarch and the grandees in every way. Then there was the introduction of regular military service under Peter the Great, whereby masters were conscripted into the ranks on the same level as their serfs. The serfs, being the first to reach officer's rank through deeds suited to men of their kind, became commanders over their masters and used to beat them with rods. The noble families were split up in the service, so that a man might never see his own kinsman.

Could virtue, then, and resolution, remain in those who from their youth had gone in fear and trembling of their commanders' rods, who could only acquire respect by acts of servility, and being each without any support from his kinsmen, remained alone, without unity or defence, liable to be subjected to violent treatment?

It is admirable that Peter the Great wished to rid religion of superstition, for indeed, superstition does not signify respect for God and his Law, but rather an affront. For to ascribe to God acts unbecoming to him is blasphemy.

In Russia, the beard was regarded as being in the image of God, and it was considered a sin to shave it off, and through this, men feel into the heresy of the Anthropomorphites. Miracles, needlessly performed, manifestations of ikons, rarely proven, were everywhere acclaimed, attracted superstitious idolatry, and provided incomes for dissolute priests.

Peter the Great strove to do away with all this. He issued decrees, ordering beards to be shaved off, and by the Spiritual Regulation, he placed a check on false miracles and manifestations and also on unseemly gatherings at shrines set up at crossways. Knowing that God's Law exists for the preservation of the human race, and not for its needless destruction, with the blessing of the Synod and the Ecumenical patriarchs, he made it permissible to eat meat on fast-days in cases of need, and especially in the Navy where, by abstaining even from fish, the men were somewhat prone to scurvy; ordering that those who voluntarily sacrificed their lives by such abstinence, should, when they duly fell ill, be thrown into the water. All this is very good, although the latter is somewhat severe.

But when did he do this? At a time when the nation was still unenlightened, and so, by taking superstition away from an unenlightened people, he removed its very faith in God's Law. This action of Peter the Great may be compared to that of an unskilled gardener who, from a weak tree, cuts off the water-shoots which absorb its sap. If it had strong roots, then this pruning would cause it to bring forth fine, fruitful branches; but since it is weak and ailing, the cutting-off of these shoots (which, through the leaves which received the external moisture, nourished the weak tree) means that it fails to produce new fruitful branches; its wounds fail to heal over with sap, and hollows are formed which threaten to destroy the tree. Thus, the cutting-off of superstitions did harm to the most basic articles of the faith; superstition decreased, but so did faith. The servile fear of Hell disappeared, but so did love of God and his Holy Law; and morals, which for lack of other enlightenment used to be improved by faith, having lost this support began to fall into dissolution.

For all the respect that I retain in my heart for this great monarch and great man, for all my feeling that the national interest itself demanded that he should have legitimate offspring as heirs to his throne—apart from the Czarevich Alexei Petrovich—I cannot refrain from censuring his divorce from his first wife, born Lopukhin, and his second marriage (with the prisoner, Catherine Alexeevna) after sending his first wife to a convent. For this example of the infringement of the sacrament of marriage, which is indissoluble in its essence, showed that it could be infringed with impunity.

Let us suppose that the monarch had strong reasons for this —which, however, I do not see, apart from his partiality for the Monses, and his wife's resistance to his new measures—but did his imitators have reasons of state for doing the like? Did Pavel Ivanovich Eguzinsky, in sending his first wife to a convent and marrying a second, born Golovin, have reasons of state which compelled him to strive to ensure his progeny by breaking God's Law? Many others followed this example, and not only from among the grandees, but even among people of low rank, such as Prince Boris Sontsev-Zasekin.

And, so through the labours and solicitude of this monarch, Russia acquired fame in Europe and influence in affairs. Her troops were organized in a proper fashion, and her fleets covered the White Sea and the Baltic; with these forces she overcame her old enemies and former conquerors, the Poles and the Swedes, and acquired important provinces and sea-ports. Sciences, arts and crafts began to flourish there, trade began to enrich her, and the Russians were transformed—from bearded men to clean-shaven men, from long-robed men to short-coated men; they became more sociable, and polite spectacles became known to them.

But at the same time, true attachment to the faith began to disappear, sacraments began to fall into disrepute, resoluteness diminished, yielding place to brazen, aspiring flattery; luxury and voluptuousness laid the foundation of their power, and hence avarice was also aroused, and, to the ruin of the laws and the detriment of the citizens, began to penetrate the law-courts.

Such was the condition with regard to morals, in which Russia was left at the death of this great monarch (despite all the barriers which Peter the Great in his own person and by his example had laid down to discourage vice).

4   *An Assessment of Peter I's Reign by a Prerevolutionary Russian Historian*

The reign of Peter I has fascinated many poets, biographers, would-be reformers, and scholars, with the result that a voluminous literature in many languages has grown on the subject. One of the most impressive assessments of Peter I, both as a man and as an iron-fisted tsar, was provided by the eminent prerevolutionary Russian historian V. O. Kliuchevskii (1841–1911) in his five-volume history of Russia entitled Kurs russkoi istorii. *The strength of Kliuchevskii's analysis centers not in the length of the treatment (there are many more verbose accounts) but in the relative balance and synthesis that succeeded in combining historical accuracy with fertile imagination. This combination elevates it into one of the best treatments of the eventful reign of the powerful tsar.*

SOURCE. Vasili Klyuchevsky, *Peter the Great*. Translated by Liliana Archibald (New York: Vintage Russian Library, 1958), pp. 254–272 Reprinted by permission of St. Martin's Press, Inc., New York, N. Y., The Macmillan Company of Canada Ltd., and Macmillan, London and Basingstoke.

. . . First of all, how did Peter become a reformer? The name of Peter makes us think of his reforms, and indeed 'Peter the Great and his reforms' has become a cliché. 'Reformer' has become his sobriquet, and the name by which he is known to history. We tend to believe that Peter I was born with the intention of reforming his country, and that he believed that this was his predestined historical mission. Nevertheless it was a long time before Peter took this view of himself. He was certainly not brought up to believe that he would reign over a state which was good for nothing, and which he would have to rebuild from top to bottom. On the contrary, he grew up knowing that he was Tsar, though a persecuted one, and that, as long as his sister and the Miloslavskys were in power, he was in danger of losing his life, and was unlikely to occupy the throne. His games of soldiers and with boats were the sports of his childhood, suggested to him by the conversations of his entourage. He realised very early that when he grew up and began to rule, he would need an army and navy, but he was, it seems, in no hurry to ask why he would need them. He only gradually realised, when he had discovered Sophia's intrigues, that he would need soldiers to control the Streltsy who supported his sister. Peter acted on the spur of the moment, and was not concerned with making plans for the future; he regarded everything he did as an immediate necessity rather than a reform, and did not notice how his actions changed both people and established systems. Even from his first foreign tour he brought back, not plans for reform, but impressions of a civilisation which he imagined he would like to introduce into Russia; and he brought back, too, a taste for the sea, that is to say, a desire to wage war against the country which had won access to the sea away from his grandfather. Indeed it was only during the last decade of his life, when the effect of his reforms was already fairly obvious, that he realised that he had done something new and spectacular. His better understanding of what he had done, however, did not help him to understand how he might act in the future. Peter thus became a reformer by accident, as it were, and even unwillingly. The war led him on and, to the end of his life, pushed him into reforming.

In the history of a country, war generally impedes reform, since foreign war and domestic reform are mutually exclusive and reform prospers best in times of peace. But in the history of Russia the correlation is different. Since a successful war has always served to secure the *status quo,* and an unsuccessful war, by provoking internal discontent, has always forced the government to review its domestic policy and introduce reforms, the government has always tried to avoid war, often to the detriment of its international position. Reforms at home were commonly achieved at the price of disaster abroad. In Peter's time the relationship between war and domestic change was different. Reforms were stimulated by the requirements of war, which indeed dictated the nature of the reforms that were undertaken. In other times the effect of war has been to force change on an unwilling government, but Peter, as he said himself, was able to learn from war what changes were needed. Unfortunately the attempt to carry on both war and reform simultaneously was unsuccessful: war slowed up reform, and reform prolonged the war because there was opposition and frequent revolt, and the forces of the nation could not be united to finish the war.

There were also interminable controversies about whether the reforms had been sufficiently elaborated, and whether they were introduced to meet the needs of the people, or had been forced on them as an unexpected act of Peter's autocratic will. In these discussions the preparations for reform were examined. It was asked whether they were deliberately calculated to bring about improvement, or were simply forced upon Peter by urgent difficulties, and were therefore only by accident measures which led to new possibilities and a new way of life. Soloviev's view was that the reforms had been prepared by Russia's past history, and even that 'they had been demanded by the people'. Some changes had been borrowed from the West and introduced in Russia as far back as Peter's grandfather, and after him by Peter's father, elder brother, and sister. Long before Peter's reign, indeed, a fairly extensive plan for reforms had been drawn up, which in many ways anticipated his own, and in some issues went further. It is true that this programme was not fully understood by medieval Russians, for it had been prepared by a few men with new ideas who had in many ways overcome the limitations of contemporary thought. Thus although changes had long been in preparation they were by no means identical with Peter's reforms. Indeed the reorganisation of Russia could have gone in one of several directions, and, given peace, could have been spread over many generations, just as, at a later period, the emancipation of the serfs was in preparation for over a century. Under Theodore and Sophia, for instance, 'politesse à la polonaise,' to use a contemporary expression, had been introduced in carriage styles and costume, and people had begun to study the Latin and Polish languages; at Court the long, wide, and ungainly medieval Russian cloak had been abolished, and, had the educational programme been taken further, the kaftan might well have been replaced by the kuntush, and the Russian dance by the polka mazurka. For the matter of that, during the century and a half after Peter's time, the medieval Russian beard was made legal again.

Peter's first reforms were adapted from the Dutch and then from the Swedish systems. Moscow was replaced by St. Petersburg, a city built on the swamps, and Peter forced the nobility and merchants to build their houses in his new capital; to achieve his purpose he transported thousands of labourers from central Russia. The reform as carried out by Peter was his personal enterprise, and though it was an enterprise of unexampled ruthlessness, it was not arbitrary and was, indeed, necessary, otherwise Russia could not have developed fast enough to deal successfully with the dangers that threatened her. Even under Catherine the Great men realised that it would have been impossible to avoid violence by leaving the modernisation of Russia to the process of time. As we have already seen, Prince Shcherbatov disapproved of Peter's reforms, and thought that their effect would be to ruin the Russian people; on the other hand, the Prince was not a defender of autocracy, and considered such a system positively harmful to a nation. Yet this part-historian, part-publicist attempted a chronological calculation in the following terms: 'In how many years, in the most favourable conditions, could Russia by herself, without the autocracy of Peter the Great, have attained her present level of education and glory?' According to his calculations, Russia would not have reached even the imperfect situation it was in at the end of the eighteenth century until, say, 1892 (i.e., one hundred years later). He assumes, of course, that Russia would be at peace, that there would be no internal troubles, and that no monarch would appear to impede the country's progress by nullifying his predecessor's efforts. And who could guarantee that there would not be in all this time a Charles XII, or Frederick II, ready to annex part of Russia and interrupt its natural development? Thus Shcherbatov, although he idealised the life of medieval Russia, was not hopeful about a successful regeneration of the country if it was 'left to the natural awakening of the people'.

It is even more difficult to estimate the influence and effect of the reforms, and this, after all, is the main problem. In order to attempt a solution it will be necessary to dissect minutely its complex component parts. So many clashes of interest, influence, and motive were involved in the Petrine reforms that we must try to distinguish between indigenous and imported ideas, between that which was foreseen and that which was arrived at haphazardly. Indeed we shall not arrive at much understanding of these reforms by looking at some simple point in isolation. We should look at three parts of this problem, first, Peter's relations with the West, second, his attitude to medieval Russia, and third, his influence on the future. In fact this last point should not be surprising, since the work of a great man commonly survives him and is even carried on by others. We must therefore include in our judgment of Peter's reforms effects which only appeared after his death. The three parts of the problem we must look into are, then, how much Peter inherited from unreformed Russia, how much he borrowed from Western Europe, and what he left Russia, or more accurately, what happened to his work after his death.

Peter inherited from medieval Russia sovereign power of a peculiar sort, and an even stranger organisation of society. At the time of the accession of the new dynasty, the sovereign power was recognised as hereditary because of its proprietorial character. As soon as it lost this proprietorial character, it was left with neither definite juridical definition nor defined scope, and began to expand or contract according to the situation and character of the monarch. Peter inherited almost complete authority, and managed to extend it even further. He created the Senate, and by so doing rid himself of the pretensions which were associated with the Boyar Duma; by abolishing the Patriarchate he also eliminated both the risk of further Nikonian scandals and of the cramping effect of the exaggerated and unctuous respect which was accorded to the Patriarch of All the Russians.

At the same time, however, it is important to remember that Peter was the first monarch to give his unlimited power a moral and political definition. Before his reign the notion of the state was identified with the person of the Tsar, in the same way as in law the owner of a house is identified with the house. Peter made a distinction between the two ideas by insisting on two oaths, one to the State, and one to the Monarch. In his ukazes he repeatedly insisted that the interests of the state were supreme, and, by so doing, made the Monarch subordinate to the state. Thus the Emperor became the chief representative of the law and the guardian of general prosperity. Peter considered himself a servant of state and country, and wrote as an official would about his victory over the Swedes at Doberau: 'From the time I *began to serve,* I have never seen such firing and such discipline among our soldiers.' Indeed the expressions *interest of the state, public good,* and *useful to the whole nation,* appear in Russian legislation for the first time I think, in Peter's time.

None the less Peter was influenced unconsciously by historical traditions in the same way that he had been unconsciously influenced by instincts. Because he thought that his reforms were in the interest of state, and for the public good, he sacrificed his son to this supreme law. The tragic death of the Tsarevitch led to the Statute of February 5th, 1722, on the law of succession. This was the first law in the history of Russian legislation to have a constitutional character. It stated: 'We issue this Statute in order to empower the ruling sovereign to specify the person to whom he wishes the heritage to pass, and to charge that person according to his judgment.' The Statute, by way of justification recalls the example of the Grand Prince Ivan III who arbitrarily disposed of the succession, appointing first his grandson and then his son to succeed him. Before Peter there had been no law of succession, and its order had been decided by custom and circumstance alone. Under the old dynasty, which looked on the state as its patrimony *(votchina)* it was customary for the father to pass on the throne to his son 'by testament'. A new system of succession, election by the Sobor (the National Assembly) was introduced in 1598. By the seventeenth century the new dynasty did not look on the state as its patrimony, but, while the hereditary system fell into disuse, the elective system was not yet established; the new dynasty was recognised as hereditary for one generation only, and in 1613 the oath was taken to Michael Romanov and his children, but no farther. In the absence of an established system, the throne was occupied sometimes after an election by the Sobor, and sometimes by presenting the heir to the people in the Square at Moscow, as was done by Tsar Alexis with the Tsarevitch Theodore, or as happened when the rebellious Streltsy and an irregular Sobor established the Dual Monarchy of Tsars Peter and Ivan.

Peter replaced the hereditary and elective systems of succession with a system of 'personal nomination' coupled with the right to revoke; that is to say, he re-established succession by testament, legalised a situation for which no law existed, and retarded constitutional law by returning to the *votchina* system of succession. The Statute of February 5th, 1722, merely reiterated the words of Ivan III who said 'To whom I wish to him shall I give the rule.' Not only did Peter irresponsibly reproduce the past in his innovations, but he also let it influence his social legislation.

Peter did nothing to change the organisation of society which had been set up by the *Ulozhenie,* nor did he alter a division of classes which was based on obligations to the state, nor did he attack serfdom. On the contrary, the old system of class obligation was complicated by the imposition of further burdens. Peter made education compulsory for the nobility; he divided the civil service from the military; he organised the urban taxpayers into a compact group first under the administration of the *zemskie izby,* and then under the town councils; and he made the merchants of the guilds, the upper urban class not only pay their ordinary taxes but form companies to lease and run factories and workshops belonging to the state. In Petrine Russia factories and workshops were not privately owned, but were state enterprises administered by a merchant of the guild who was compelled to do so. Nevertheless there were compensations, for the merchants, manufacturers, and workshop superintendents were granted one of the privileges of the nobility, that of buying villages with serfs to work in the factory or workshop. Peter did not alter the nature of serfdom but did modify its structure: the many types of serfdom, each with a different legal and economic position, were combined, and one class of taxable serfs was the result. Some of the 'free idlers' were registered as inferior urban citizens, so that 'idlers shall take themselves to trade in order that nobody shall be without an occupation'; others were conscripted, or forced into bondage. Thus Peter, by abolishing the intermediate classes, continued the work of simplification started by the *Ulozhenie;* and his legislation forced the members of the intermediate classes into one or other of the main classes. It was in Peter's time that Russian society was organised in the fashion planned in seventeenth-century legislation; after Peter's reforms Russian society was divided into clearly defined classes, and every class was burdened with complicated and weighty duties. Peter's attitude to the political and social régime of old Russia, which we have discussed in other connections, has now been made clear. He neither disturbed old foundations, nor built new ones, but altered existing arrangements by separating classes previously combined, or combining classes hitherto divided. Both society and the institutions of government were made more vigorous by these changes, and the state benefited from their greater activity.

What was Peter's attitude to Western Europe? He had inherited the precept 'Do everything after the example of foreign countries', that is to say Western European countries. This precept combines large doses of despondency, a lack of confidence in Russia's strength, and self-denial. How did Peter interpret this precept? What did he think of Russian relations with Western Europe? Did he see in Western Europe a model to imitate or a master who could be dismissed at the end of the lesson? Peter thought that the biggest loss suffered by Muscovy in the seventeenth century had been the Baltic littoral, by which Russia was deprived of contact with the civilised nations of the West. Yet why did he want this contact? Peter has often been accused of being a blind and inveterate Westerner who admired everything foreign, not because it was better than the Russian, but because it was unlike anything Russian; and it was believed that he wanted rather to assimilate Russia to Western Europe than to make

Russia resemble Western Europe. It is difficult to believe that as sensible a man as Peter was troubled by such fantasies.

We have already seen how, in 1697, he had travelled incognito with the Great Embassy, with the intention of acquiring general technical knowledge and recruiting West European naval technicians. Indeed it was for technical reasons that the West was necessary to Peter. He was not a blind admirer of the West; on the contrary, he mistrusted it, and was not deluded into thinking that he could establish cordial relations with the West, for he knew that the West mistrusted his country, and was hostile to it. On the anniversary in 1724 of the Peace of Nystadt, Peter wrote that all countries had tried hard to exclude the Russians from knowledge in many subjects, and particularly military affairs, but somehow the countries had let information on military affairs escape them, as if their sight had been obscured, 'as if everything was veiled in front of their eyes.' Peter found this a miracle from God, and ordered the miracle to be forcefully expressed in the forthcoming celebrations 'and boldly set out, for there is a lot of meaning here', by which he meant that the subject was very suggestive of ideas. Indeed we would gladly believe the legend which has come down to us, that Peter once said, as Osterman records it: 'We need Europe for a few decades; later on we must turn our back on it.' Thus for Peter association with Europe was only a means to an end, and not an end in itself.

What did Peter hope to gain from a rapprochement? Before answering this question, we must remember why Peter sent scores of young Russians to study abroad, and ask what type of foreigner he attracted to Russia. The young Russian was sent to study mathematics, the natural sciences, naval architecture, and navigation; the foreigners who came to Russia were officers, naval architects, sailors, artisans, mining engineers, and later on jurists and specialists in administration and finance. With their help Peter introduced into Russia useful technical knowledge and skills lacked by the Russians. Russia had no regular army: he created one. It had no fleet: he built one. It had no convenient maritime commercial outlet: with his army and navy he took the eastern littoral of the Baltic. Mining was barely developed, and manufacturing hardly existed, yet by Peter's death there were more than two hundred factories and workshops in the country. The establishment of industry depended on technical knowledge, so Peter founded a naval academy, and many schools of navigation, medicine, artillery and engineering, including some where Latin and mathematics were taught, as well as nearly fifty elementary schools in provincial and sub-provincial main towns. He even provided nearly fifty garrison schools for soldiers' children. There was insufficient revenue, so Peter more than trebled it. There was no rationally organised administration capable of managing this new and complicated business, so foreign experts were called on to help to create a new central administration.

The above is, of course, an incomplete account of Peter's achievements, but it does show what he hoped to do with the help of Western Europe. Peter called on Western Europe to work and train Russians in financial and administrative affairs, and in the technical sciences. He did not want to borrow the results of Western technique, but wanted to appropriate the skill and knowledge, and build industries on the Western European model. The intelligent Russian of the seventeenth century realised that it was essential to increase Russia's productive capacity, by exploiting the country's natural and virgin riches, in order that the increased requirements of the state might be more easily met. Peter shared this point of view, and gave effect to it as did nobody before or after him, and he is therefore unique in the history of Russia. In foreign policy he concentrated on solving the Baltic problem.

It would be difficult to assess the value of the many industries he introduced. The evidence of the increased wealth was not a higher standard of living, but increased revenue. All increased earnings were, in fact, used to pay for the war. Peter's intention had been general economic reform, but the only evidence of success was the improved financial position. When Pososhkov wrote to Peter in 1724 that 'it was a great and difficult business to enrich all the people', he was not explaining a theory but sadly stating what he, and many others, had observed to be fact. In Peter's time men worked not for themselves but for the state, and after working better and harder than their fathers, probably died a great deal poorer. Peter did not leave the state in debt for one kopeck, nor did he waste a working day at the expense of future

generations. On the contrary, he left his descendants rich re-
serves to draw on. His superiority lies in the fact that he was a
creditor of the future, not a debtor. We will pursue this point later when we discuss the results of his reform. Were we to draw up
a balance sheet of Peter's activities, excluding those affecting
Russia's security and international position, but including those
affecting the people's welfare, we would find that his great economic ambitions (which were the basis for his reforms) failed in
their purpose, and, in fact, their only success was financial.

Thus Peter took from the old Russia the absolute power, the
law, and the class structure; from the West he borrowed the
technical knowledge required to organise the army, the navy, the
economy, and the government. Where then was the revolution
which renewed or transformed the Russian way of life, which introduced not only new institutions, but new principles (whether
they were good or bad, is for the moment, immaterial). Peter's
contemporaries, however, thought that the reforms were revolutionary, and they communicated their opinion to their descendants. But the reforms did not stop the Russians from doing
things in their own way, and it was not the innovations that agi-
tated them so much as the methods Peter used. Some of the
results of the reforms were only felt in the future, and their significance was certainly not understood by everyone, and contemporaries anyhow only knew the effect the reforms had on them.
Some reactions, however, were immediate, and these Peter had
to account for.

The reforms were influenced not only by Peter's personality,
but by wars and internecine struggles. Although the war had
caused Peter to introduce reforms, it had an adverse influence on
their development and success, because they were effected in an
atmosphere of confusion usually consequent on war. The difficulties and demands of war forced Peter do to [sic] everything
hastily. The requirements of war imposed a nervous and feverish
tempo on the reforms, and an unhealthily fast pace. Peter's military preoccupations did not leave him time for critical analysis of
a situation or careful consideration of his orders and the conditions in which they would be carried out. He could not wait pa-
tiently for natural improvement; he required rapid action and
immediate results; at every delay or difficulty he would goad the

officials with the threats which he used so often that they lost their power. Indeed for any offence against the law, such as petitioning the Tsar without going through the proper authorities, or felling an oak, or even a spruce, or failing to appear at a nobleman's review, or buying or selling clothes of the old Russian pattern, Peter ordered confiscation of property, loss of civil rights, the knout, forced labour, the gallows, or physical and civil death. This extravaganza of punishments produced an increase in wrongdoing, or a general feeling of oppression and perplexity that resulted in neurasthenia. General-Admiral Apraxin, one of Peter's most eager collaborators, has vividly described this state of mind in a letter written in 1716 to Makarov, the Tsar's personal secretary: 'Verily, in all affairs we wander like blind men, not knowing what to do; everywhere there is great agitation, we do not know to whom to turn, or what to do about it for the future; there is no money anywhere, and everything will come to a stop.'

Moreover the reforms were evolved in the middle of bitter internal struggles, which often burst into violence; four terrible uprisings and three or four conspiracies were directed against Peter's innovations, and all appealed to people's feeling for antiquity, to the old prejudices and ideas. These troubles reinforced Peter's hostility to the old customs and habits which to him symbolised the prejudices and ideas of the past. The political education he had received was primarily responsible for this hostility. From his childhood he had witnessed the struggle which had divided Russian society from the beginning of the seventeenth century. On one side were the advocates of change who turned to the West for help, and on the other were the political and religious Old Believers. The beards and clothes of the Old Believers were symbols adopted expressly to distinguish them from the Western Europeans. In themselves these trivialities of dress were no obstacle to reform, but the sentiments and convictions of their wearers were certainly an obstacle. Peter took the side of the innovators, and hotly opposed these trifling practices, as well as the ancient traditions that the Russian insisted on observing. The memories of childhood were responsible for the Tsar's excessive attention to these details. He associated these symbols with the risings of the Streltsy and the Old Believers. To him, the beard worn by an Old Believer was not a detail of masculine appearance, but, like the long-skirted coat, the mark of a political attitude, the spirit of opposition. He wanted to have clean-shaven subjects wearing foreign clothes, in the belief that this would help them to behave like Western Europeans.

When he returned to Moscow in 1698, on hearing of the rising of the Streltsy, one of the first things he did was to shave beards, cut the long coats of his entourage, and introduce wigs. It is hard to imagine the difficulties of legislation, and the uproar that was produced by this forcible transformation of costume and fashion. The clergy and the peasants, however, were not affected by these measures; they retained their class privilege of remaining orthodox and conservative. In January 1700, the order that, by next Shrovetide, everyone else was to appear in a Hungarian kaftan, was proclaimed with rolling drums in streets and squares. In 1701 a new ukaze was issued: men were to wear a jacket in the French or Saxon style, a waistcoat, breeches, gaiters, boots, and caps, in the German style; women were to wear bonnets, petticoats, skirts and shoes, in the German style. Censors of dress and beards were posted at the gates of towns, with instructions to fine the wearers of beards and illegal dress, which was to be torn to pieces. Noblemen who appeared at reviews with beards and moustaches were unmercifully beaten. The bearded Old Believers were compelled to wear special clothes, while their wives, though spared by nature from paying a fine on beards, had, because of their husbands' beards, to wear long robes and peaked bonnets. Merchants who sold old-fashioned clothes were knouted, had their property confiscated, and were sent to forced labour.

All this might be amusing if it were not so contempible [sic]! It was the first time that Russian legislation abandoned its serious tone and concerned itself with trifles better left to hairdressers and tailors. These caprices aroused much hostility among the people. These petty annoyances explain the disproportion, which is so striking between the sacrifices involved in Peter's internal reforms, and their actual achievements. Indeed it is astonishing to find the number of difficulties that had to be overcome to achieve even modest results. Even Peter's fervent admirer, Pososhkov, vigorously and appropriately described the difficulties

Peter had to overcome, Peter who alone pulled the chariot of state up the hill, while millions pulled in the opposite direction. Another of Peter's admirers, one Nartov, a turner, wrote in his memoirs of everything 'that has been conceived against this monarch, what he underwent, and the hurt he suffered'. Peter went against the wind, and by his rapid motion increased the resistance he encountered. There were contradictions in his actions which he was unable to resolve, discordances which could not be harmonised.

As he grew older, and left his unruly youth behind him, he became more anxious than any other Tsar had been for the welfare of his people, and he directed the whole of his forceful energy to its improvement. His devotion attracted such intelligent men as Bishop Mitrophan, Nepluev, Pososhkov, and Nartov, who understood what it was that was driving Peter on, and who became his fervent admirers. Nartov, for instance, in calling Peter a god, added 'without fear we call him father; he has taught us truth and a noble fearlessness'.

Unfortunately Peter's methods alienated those indifferent to his reforms, and turned them into stubborn opponents. Peter used force, not example, and relied on mens' instincts and not on their moral impulses. Governing his country from the post-chaise and stagehouse, he thought always of business, never of people, and, sure of his own power, he neglected to pay sufficient attention to the passive resistance of the masses. A reforming zeal and a faith in autocracy were Peter's two hands; unfortunately one hand paralysed the energy of the other. Peter thought that he could supplement the lack of proper resources by using power to urge people on, and aimed at the impossible. As a result the officials became so intimidated and inefficient that they lost their ability to do what they were normally quite capable of doing. As Peter, for all his zeal, was unable to use people's strength, so the people, in their state of inert and passive resistance, were unable to appreciate Peter's efforts.

Thus without exaggerating or belittling the work of Peter the Great, we can summarise it as follows: the reforms were brought on by the essential requirements of state and people; the need for reform was understood by an authoritative, intelligent, energetic, and talented individual, one of those who, for no apparent reason, appear from time to time. Further, he was gifted, and, animated by a sense of duty, was resolved 'not to spare his life in the service of his country'. When Peter came to the throne, Russia was not in an advantageous position compared with other European countries. Towards the end of the sixteenth century the Russians had created a great state, which was one of the largest in Europe; in the seventeenth century, however, it began to fail in moral and material strength. Peter's reforms did not aim directly at changing the political, social, or moral order, nor did they aim at forcing Russian life into an alien Western European pattern. The reforms only aimed at providing the Russian State and people with Western European intellectual and material resources, so that Russia might take its just position in Europe, and its people increase their productive capacity. But Peter had to do all this in a hurry, in the middle of a dangerous and bitter war, by using constraint at home; he had to struggle with the rapacity of his rascally officials, a gross landed nobility, and the prejudices and fears instilled by an ignorant clergy. The first reforms had been modest and limited, aimed only at reconstructing the army and developing the financial resources of the state; later, however, the reforms were the occasion for an obstinate battle which disturbed the existing pattern of living, and upset society. Started and carried through by the sovereign, the people's usual leader, the reforms were undertaken in conditions of upheaval, almost of revolution, not because of their objects but because of their methods, and by the impressions they made on the nerves and imaginations of the people. Perhaps it was more of a shock than a revolution, but the shock was the unforeseen and unintended consequence of the reforms.

Let us end by giving our opinion of Peter's reforms. The contradition in his work, his errors, his hesitations, his obstinacy, his lack of judgment in civil affairs, his uncontrollable cruelty, and, on the other hand, his wholehearted love of his country, his stubborn devotion to his work, the broad, enlightened outlook he brought to bear on it, his daring plans conceived with creative genius and concluded with incomparable energy, and finally the success he achieved by the incredible sacrifices of his people and himself, all these different characteristics make it difficult to paint one painting. Moreover they explain the diverse impression he made on people; he sometimes provoked unqualified admiration, sometimes unqualified hostility. Generally the criticism prevailed because even his good actions were accompanied by disgusting methods.

Peter's reforms were the occasion for a struggle between the despot and the people's inertia. The Tsar hoped to arouse the energies and initiative of a society subdued by serfdom with the menace of his power, and strove, with the help of the noblemen, the oppressors of serfs, to introduce into Russia the European sciences and education which were essential to social progress. He also wanted the serf, while remaining a serf, to act responsibly and freely. The conjunction of despotism and liberty, of civilisation and serfdom, was a paradox which was not resolved in the two centuries after Peter. It is true that Russians of the eighteenth century tried to reconcile the Petrine reforms with humanitarian instincts, and Prince Shcherbatov, who was opposed to autocracy, devoted a treatise to explaining and even justifying Peter's vices and arbitrary conduct. Shcherbatov recognized that the enlightment introduced into Russia by Peter benefited the country, and attacked Peter's critics on the grounds that they themselves had been the recipients of a culture, bestowed on them by the autocracy, which permitted them to distinguish the evils inherent in the autocratic system. Peter's faith in the miraculous power of education, and his respect for scientific knowledge, inspired the servile with little understanding of the meaning of civilisation; this understanding grew slowly, and was eventually transformed into a desire for truth and liberty.

Autocracy as a political principle is in itself odious. Yet we can reconcile ourselves to the individual who exercises this unnatural power when he adds self-sacrifice to it, and, although an autocrat, devotes himself unsparingly to the public good, risking destruction even on difficulties caused by his own work. We reconcile ourselves in the same way to the impetuous showers of spring, which strip branches from the trees, but none the less refresh the air, and by their downpour bring on the growth of the new seed.

5   An Assessment of Peter I's Modernization in Soviet Historiography

Generally speaking, the reign of Peter I has received favorable treatment in Soviet historiography. Soviet scholars have praised the iron-fisted tsar for creating a strong army and navy, for his efforts in behalf of education and industry, and for his measures designed to eliminate the country's backwardness. Soviet scholars view these achievements as "positive" and as being of "great historical importance." By "historical importance" they mean that thanks to Peter I's policies Russia emerged as a major military power in Europe, and without her participation "no important European problem could now be settled." The following selection was prepared for Soviet university students and was published in 1956.

Reforms of the first quarter of the eighteenth century affected all areas of state administration. Changes in the structure of the state apparatus were outlined already at the end of the seventeenth century. At the start of reorganizations the *prikaz* system was preserved; in fact, alongside the old prikazes new ones appeared (Preobrazhenskii, Military Affairs, and others). Without formally dissolving the *Boiar Duma,* Peter I gradually created new organs of administration during the first years of the Northern War. Of vital political significance was the *Konziliia* [Council] of Ministers that usually met in the Tsar's Inner Office. Membership of the Council consisted of heads of important prikazes and of military commanders. The Tsar's Personal Chancellery—"the Cabinet"—played a vital role in administering state affairs. All matters of anti-state transgressions were handled by the Preobrazhenskii prikaz.

Systematic reorganization of state apparatus began in 1708–9

SOURCE. M. V. Nechkina, et. al., ed. *Istoriia SSSR s drevneishikh vremen do 1861 g.* [A History of the USSR From Ancient Times to 1861] (Moscow: Gospolitizdat, 1956), Vol. I, pp. 442–455. Translation by Basil Dmytryshyn.

with the division of the country into gubernias. Governors had
been appointed at an earlier date to administer special areas of
the state (A. D. Menshikov, for example, was appointed Governor of Ingria, which had been conquered during the early stages
of the Northern War). In 1708, at the height of popular discontent in the south, to establish strong local authority to struggle
with the anti-feudal rebellions, the entire country was divided
into 8 gubernias (Moscow, St. Petersburg, Kiev, Smolensk, Archangel, Kazan, Azov, and Siberia). Each was presided over by
a governor with broad powers and with the right to command local military units. The gubernia reforms strengthened the domination of nobles in local areas. Later the Astrakhan, Nizhnii-
Novgorod, and Riga Gubernias were created, while that of Smolensk was abolished.

In 1711, before the Prut campaign, Peter I issued an ukaz
creating the Senate, which initially consisted of nine members. In
contrast to the Boiar Duma, membership of the Senate consisted
not only of representatives of the aristocracy, but also of high officials from among the nobles who were close to the Tsar. The
Senate was the supreme organ of administration, but not advi-
sory-legislative as was the Boiar Duma. Its competence covered
justice, finances, military, foreign trade, and like matters. All vital state acts were henceforth issued in the name of the Tsar's
authority ("personal" ukazes). In its relation with local authorities, as well as for the purpose of controlling them, the Senate included in its midst two commissars from each gubernia. Staff-
officers were appointed at first, and to control the activity of the
Senate the post of Procurator-General was set up in 1722. The
Procurator General appointed local procurators to supervise the
activity of local administration. Within the Senate the post of
Ober-fiscal was established, whose task was to report on abuses.
Local fiscals were subject to the Ober-fiscal.

With the establishment of Colleges, initially all of their presidents were members of the Senate. This led to abuses of authority. Senators shielded one another and whitewashed the activities
of their Colleges before the Senate. Peter I then acknowledged
that this order was "prepared in haste," and all presidents of
Colleges, except Military, Admiralty, and Foreign Affairs, were
excluded from the Senate.

To supervise the proper service of nobles and their children, there was created the post of Heraldmeister. The order of service was determined by the Table of Ranks of 1722. To review complaints against actions of Colleges and to submit the complaints to the Senate, the post of Reketmeister General was established.

The reform of the central administration was completed with the establishment of Colleges. In 1718, in place of the prikazes that existed in the seventeenth century, twelve Colleges were set up. The College of Foreign Affairs dealt with the problems of foreign policy; Military College—with land forces; Admiralty College—with naval forces; Justice College—with civil courts; Kamer College—with the collection of state revenues; Shtats College—with state expenditures; Revizion College—with the auditing of revenues and expenditures; Berg College—with mining and metallurgical industries; Manufaktur College—with other branches of industry; Votchina College—with the ownership of land by nobles; Chief Magistrate—with the administration of cities; and the Holy Synod or Spiritual College—with the administration of church affairs. The Colleges differed from the old prikazes by the principle of collectivity in reviewing and deciding matters, and also by the fact that among the Colleges there were more clearly distributed the divisions of state administration. Each College was headed by a president, assisted by vice-presidents, several counsellors and assessors, and an office of staff officials (collegial secretary, archivist, and others). To guide the work of Colleges there was prepared, and, in 1720, implemented, a General Regulation. The terms of the General Regulation, which served as a guide for preparing regulations of each of the Colleges, were to a large extent borrowed from foreign (primarily Swedish) legislation, but were modified on Peter I's order "to suit this state" (i.e., Russia). . . .

In 1722 an ukaz on succession was issued. By its terms the monarch appointed his successor according to his wishes.

Local administration under Peter I underwent further change. In 1713 nobles received the right to elect in gubernias eight to twelve *Landrat*s (counsellors) to aid governors. In 1715 gubernias were subdivided into parts, each containing 5,536 farmsteads. The parts were administered by the Landrats and by the commanders of local garrisons. The parts were abolished in

1719, and gubernias were divided into 50 provinces, each headed by a voevoda who was supervised either by Colleges or the Senate. In each province there were established posts of: *Kamer* and *Rentmeister* (in charge of finances); *Proviantmeister* (in charge of food collection); and *Waldmeister* (to supervise forests). Provinces were divided into districts headed by Land Commissars selected from among local nobles or retired officers. These commissars and other officials were appointed by the Kamer and Shtats Colleges.

After soul tax was introduced, military units were quartered in local places to supervise its collection. This in turn led to the organization of new administrative-financial districts—known as Regimental Districts. The collection of soul tax was entrusted to a special Land Commissar selected from among nobles at their local meeting.

The development of industry and trade led to the strengthening of the upper echelons of the city. In fiscal interests, and to provide greater rights for merchants, a city reform was introduced in 1699. City population was excluded from the jurisdiction of the voevodas, and placed under the supervision of Burgermeisters elected by town inhabitants. Local Burgermeisters were under the jurisdiction of the Burgermeister Hall or the *Ratusha* in Moscow, which was also empowered to collect all indirect taxes (customs, drink, etc.) from the city population.

In 1720 the Chief Magistrate was founded in Petrograd to supervise city magistrates. The rich merchant I. Isaev was appointed Vice President of the Chief Magistrate. The reform of town administration protected merchants from the arbitrariness of local administration. Magistrates, who consisted of elected Burgermeisters and counsellors, supervised the collection of taxes and justice over town inhabitants. Town population was divided into "regular" and "irregular" citizens. "Irregular" were those who had no property. "Regular" were divided into two guilds: the first consisted of merchants and industrialists; the second of petty merchants and craftsmen. Only "regular" citizens enjoyed the right to elect local magistrates.

During Peter I's reign a church reform was introduced. After the death of Patriarch Adrian in 1700 no new patriarch was appointed, and temporary administration of the church was assigned to the "Protector of the Patriarchal See," the Metropolitan of Riazan, Stefan Iavorskii. To break the opposition of conservative clergy to the reforms undertaken and to subject the church to the state at last, in 1721 the Patriarchate was abolished and the Special Spiritual College—the Holy Governing Synod—was set up. It was presided over by a president from among the high clergy. The activity of the Synod, its functions, and obligations, were determined by the Spiritual Regulation prepared by Archbishop Theophan Prokopovich. The abolishment of the Patriarchate was justified in the Spiritual Regulation by political dangers that stemmed from attempts to equate spiritual authority of the Patriarch with the supreme power of the sovereign, as well as by advantages of collegial over personal administration of church affairs.

After the death of the Synod's President, Stefan Iavorskii, in 1722, Peter I did not appoint a successor, and entrusted the supervision of the Synod's activity to the Ober-Procurator of the Synod.

The government tried to register lands belonging to church institutions and monasteries. Monastery estates were under the jurisdiction of the Monastery Prikaz and a sizable portion of their revenues went to the state treasury. The number of monks in each monastery was also set. Establishment of new monasteries was prohibited. None of this prevented the government from using the Orthodox Church as a weapon of its policy. . . .

Reorganization of the central state apparatus made under Peter I created a structure of government organs that without important changes remained in effect till the last quarter of the eighteenth century. As a result of these changes, absolutism in the country was strengthened. During Peter I's reign the absolute monarchy became at last a reality. It was based on the official-bureaucratic apparatus of the administration and on the regular army, which was required not only to defend the country but also to suppress popular movements. The church was transformed into a loyal servant of absolutism. . . .

The military organization of Russia at the end of the seventeenth century failed to meet the needs of an absolute state. Creation of a regular army was dictated by the tasks of foreign policy and by the growth of military technology. Sharp increase of class struggle in the country also demanded creation of a regular, well-trained army that would be separated from the mass of the population.

The military reform, as well as other reorganization schemes of the government, was set in motion already in the seventeenth century, with the creation of regiments based on a "foreign model." In spite of all these attempts to reorganize the army, wars of the second half of the seventeenth century revealed great shortcomings in military affairs. The few factories could not satisfy the needs of the army in arms and supplies. The equipment of the military was to a considerable degree of a differing type and quality and for the most part obsolete. Training was weak and inadequate.

Already in his youth Peter showed serious interest in military and naval affairs. He participated in the construction of a "play fortress" named Preshburg on the bank of the Iauza River, and on Pereiaslav Lake a small fleet was built. From Peter's play soldiers, emerged the Preobrazhenskii and Semenovskii Regiments that became the nucleus of the Russian regular army. To train his regiments Peter conducted major maneuvers, which revealed the superiority of regular training of his soldiers over "untrained" actions of the streltsy. While he gradually improved the organization of his armies, Peter organized the "bombardier company" and the military-engineering command in 1695–6, during the Azov campaign. In the Voronezh Yards was constructed a fleet consisting of two sailships armed with 36 guns, 23 galleys, and 4 fireships. These measures helped greatly in capturing Azov in 1696. The experience of the Azov campaign also showed the need to study seriously contemporary military science and technology.

During foreign travel in 1696–8 Peter and his "volunteers" diligently studied naval affairs and ship construction, artillery, military engineering, organization and tactics of infantry and cavalry, and other related problems. Superior achievements in military matters in European countries were creatively utilized in the building of the Russian regular army.

In 1699–1700, before the start of the Northern War, from tax paying people (from 1705 on they were called recruits) and from "volunteers" (willingly registered), 27 military regiments were organized in Moscow. These regiments received uniform equipment, uniform weapons and supplies, and were grouped into 3 divisions. To train soldiers and officers, and to introduce "proper discipline" in these regiments, Peter and his generals, A. M. Golovin and A. A. Weide, prepared basic rules which contained embryonic ideas that were subsequently developed in depth and in detail in the Military *Ustav* [Code] of 1716.

The defeat at Narva on November 19, 1700 provided new impetus for adopting more energetic measures in the re-organization of the armed forces. The cavalry of the nobility was abolished, and was replaced by regular cavalry (consisting at first of 10 dragoon regiments) with uniform organization, arms, and tactics. In place of obsolete diverse gauge artillery of the seventeenth century, the Armament Court and the new Ural works began casting precise weapons determined by the Tsar himself (howitzers, cannons, mortars). This represented a new serious policy in artillery matters. In 1701 an artillery regiment was organized. On the Neva River and its tributaries a ship and galley fleet was constructed energetically in accordance with all rules of contemporary naval art. The problem of administering and supplying the army and the fleet was centered in the Prikaz of Military Affairs and in the Admiralty. From 1702 on, the rank-and-file of the army and the fleet was filled by systematically conducted recruit levies (from a designated number of settlements and peasant households).

The development of native military production played the decisive role in strengthening the defense capability of the Russian state. The production of hand guns reached tens of thousands of pieces per year, and fully satisfied the needs of the army. In Moscow alone, from 1700 to 1708, 1000 weapons of improved quality were produced, while the total figure of produced weapons during Peter's rule was over 10,000.

The rich experience during the Northern War enabled, during the war itself, the improvement of weapons, organization, and tactics of the army and of the fleet. On the eve of the battle of Poltava the entire army was equipped with hand rifles with flint lock and bayonet, and with contemporary artillery. Infantry and cavalry regiments were regrouped into brigades and divisions. Grenadier regiments armed with hand grenades in addition to ri-

fles and bayonets were organized. At the head of the army was
Peter, assisted by such experienced and able Russian generals as
A. D. Menshikov, B. P. Sheremetev, N. I. Repnin, and others,
who led the Russian army to a famous victory at Poltava. From
among Peter's Russian associates emerged famous naval officers
and shipbuilders such as F. M. Apraxin, N. A. Seniavin, and
others; artillery officers and military engineers such as Ia. V.
Bruce, G. G. Skorniakov-Pisarev, and V. D. Korchmin.
Hundreds of nobles studied military affairs in schools Peter
founded.

With great strain a regular navy was organized, which demonstrated its superiority over the Swedish fleet in battles at Gangut
and Grengham. In the yards of the Baltic fleet alone, from 1702
to 1725 there were built 39 battle ships, 19 frigates, 250 galleys,
and many small vessels. The total number of ships and small vessels built during Peter's reign was 895. Naval history knew no
similar examples before. On the basis of their sea-going qualities
(speed and maneuverability) new ships equalled those built in
the yards of a number of West European countries.

The regular army which Peter I created was the army of a
feudal-serf state and had a clearly expressed class composition.
Rank-and-file soldiers and sailors were recruited from among the
peasants and settlement population; with only rare exception officers were nobles. Nevertheless this army, replenished by an obligatory recruiting system, was a national army in its composition. In this it differed from the mercenary armies of a number
of Western states. Leading military ideas of Peter and his associates found clear expression in the Military Code of 1716 and
in the Naval Code of 1720. Both were formulated on Peter's
own initiative and with his close participation. The Russian regular army and the fleet received battle experience in the Northern
War. . . .

Russian national culture of the first quarter of the eighteenth
century gained a number of significant achievements. The prereq-
uisites for cultural development lay in economic development,
while the successes were centered in the realm of foreign policy.

After he returned from his first foreign trip in 1697–8, Peter
introduced, among other major measures, a reform in chronology and calendar. Chronology based on the so-called birth of

Christ—that changed the New Year from September 1 to January 1 (by the Julian calendar) —was introduced in 1700.

The chief attention was given to the founding of schools and school training to prepare officer cadres for the army and the fleet.

In 1699 a gunnery school was founded in Moscow. In 1701 an artillery school was opened. In 1701 in the Sucharev Tower building a navigation school was opened, where 300 students studied. In 1707, at the military hospital in Moscow, a Medical School was opened. In 1715 in Petrograd the Naval Academy was organized—the second in Europe (after France). Engineer schools were founded in Moscow and Petersburg to train military engineers. At the Voronezh Yards, the Petersburg Admiralty, in Kazan, Astrakhan, Nizhnii-Novgorod, and other places, new schools for shipbuilders were established; while at major industries craft schools were founded. Young nobles studied navigation and pilotage in Petrograd, Reval, and Narva. In several towns Cipher Schools were opened to teach general education.

Peter left the task of theological training to the Slavonic-Greek-Latin Academy. All other schools were given an exclusively secular and professional outlook. Students were required to participate in practical work (in laboratories, in artillery firing ranges, aboard ships, and in forts).

An acute demand for technical intelligentsia forced the opening of school doors to individuals of non-noble origin. Children of townsmen, gunners, lesser clerks, and others, who entered these schools, demonstrated a great desire to learn. Severe discipline prevailed in schools. Students were subject to corporal punishment and fines for infractions.

Textbooks were published for those who studied. In 1703 appeared "Arithmetic—or a Study of Numbers" by L. F. Magnitskii, who first introduced in Russia Arabic numerals in place of old letters. His "Arithmetic" represents a kind of encyclopedia of mathematical knowledge, geodesy, astronomy, and navigation. Later appeared new teaching aids by Magnitskii, by an English astronomer-mathematician, A. D. Farvanson; by G. G. Skorniakov-Pisarev, and others. For Cipher Schools, located in gubernias, was published a textbook—"The Primer for Boys," by F. Prokopovich.

After they completed the course, students were required to take stiff examinations. Those who passed them successfully were sent as officers to the army or the fleet, as draftsmen in laboratories, as engravers in printing establishments, as masters in factories and shipyards, and as petty clerks in offices. The most capable students were appointed teachers in schools. Russians easily mastered knowledge.

At the close of the Northern War, when the critical need for cadres had passed, only nobles were admitted to schools.

In the first quarter of the eighteenth century publishing activity was elevated to a new height. In Moscow, alongside the old Publishing Court, a "secular" printing press was founded to print texts, engravings, and maps. In St. Petersburg, four new printing presses appeared—one for "foreign languages." In 1703 the first Russian newspaper, *Vedomosti*, made its appearance. It published news about domestic developments and foreign affairs. Of vital significance in the development of Russian culture was the reform of the alphabet. In 1708, in place of Church-Slavonic, a new secular type was introduced, which, with slight changes, exists to date. This reform made the book more available to the reader and enabled the introduction of national language into the literature.

In the course of 26 years (1699–1725) about 600 books were published in Russia, plus news bulletins, instructions, etc. Book stores were opened in Moscow, Petersburg, and other cities to distribute books.

Translations from foreign languages were made—especially those books that had a scientific content. Timofei Fedorov translated a book about artillery. Vasili Suvorov, father of A. V. Suvorov, translated from the French a book by the famous engineer, Beauplan, entitled "The Proper Way to Fortify Cities." The great Russian military leader later studied that book.

Among famous and talented translators were B. Volkov, P. Postnikov, F. P. Polikarpov, K. Zotov, and others. Peter followed their work carefully and insisted that they translate into spoken Russian.

Some Russian works were translated into foreign languages ("A Discourse" by P. P. Shafirov, on the causes of the war with Sweden; "Spiritual Regulations" and "On Monarchical Power"

by F. Prokopovich and others). A map of the Caspian Sea, prepared by Russian cartographers, received high praise by the French Academy of Sciences.

The growth of cultural needs of the society was also reflected in libraries. In 1714 foundations were laid down to a library that subsequently emerged as the Academy of Sciences Library. Stocked with private libraries and books purchased abroad, in time this library was transformed into a major depository of books. Large libraries belonged to such private individuals as A. D. Menshikov, B. P. Sheremetev, F. Prokopovich, A. A. Matveev, V. N. Tatishchev and others.

In the realm of manufacturing, during the first quarter of the eighteenth century, new technology received wide application. While manual labor was employed in the construction of factories, shipyards, canals, and harbors, use was made of hydraulic lifting machines and pulleys. Much evidence exists indicating that Russians successfully mastered not only contemporary technology, but made their own contributions to its further development.

Thus, blast furnaces in iron mills in the Urals were superior in construction and productivity to English furnaces. Soldier Ia. Batishev invented a machine for water turning of gun barrels and bayonets. A great many discoveries and innovations were made in the military field. Ia. B. Bruce discovered a means to accelerate artillery firing; V. D. Korchmin constructed a cannon carriage; a peasant, Efim Nikonov, submitted a project of "an underwater vessel"; and an unknown inventor developed a project of constructing a military chariot, to be driven by horses, shielded by adjustable "sickles" and a mounted cannon on a pivot yoke.

Great contributions to the development of Russian technology were made by such outstanding engineers as V. N. Tatishchev and V. de Gennin.

Geological prospecting for useful minerals gained considerable popularity. The foundation was laid for prospecting for coal in the Donets Basin. Much attention was devoted to cartographical and hydrographical works. Russian hydrographers prepared maps and sketches of the Azov, Caspian, Baltic, and White Seas. Early in the eighteenth century, S. V. Remezov, a petty official in Tobolsk, prepared on 24 sheets a "Sketch Book" of Siberia. In 1719, geodecists I. M. Evreinov and F. Luzhin were sent with an instruction: to proceed to Kamchatka to ascertain whether America and Asia were "joined." The expedition reached the Kurile Islands, which it placed on the map. At about this time T. K. Kirillov began preparing a summary "Atlas of the Russian Empire," whose first volume appeared in 1732. In 1725, three weeks before his death, Peter signed an ukaz authorizing V. Bering's expedition, whose aim was to discover where Kamchatka "joined America." Peter Postnikov, son of an official of the Posolskii prikaz, was one of the first Russians to receive a degree of doctor of medicine and philosophy.

During the first quarter of the eighteenth century the foundation was laid for gathering of natural-scientific collections, historical sources, and museum objects. The assembled "rarities" in the "Kunstkamer" laid the foundation for the first museum in Russia; the assembled ship models in the "Model-Kamer" laid the groundwork for the Naval Museum; and the assembled old weapons served as the beginning of the Artillery Museum. On Peter's order, throughout the state were collected ancient manuscripts and books, "old inscriptions," coins, and "curious letters." A copy was prepared from an old Russian chronicle, beautifully decorated with miniatures, that was preserved in Königsberg.

A very valuable historical work was the two-volume "History of the Swedish War," written with Peter I's participation and published at the end of the eighteenth century by M. M. Shcherbatov, under the title "A Journal or A Daily Notebook of Emperor Peter the Great." A. I. Mankiev, a secretary of the Russian envoy to Sweden, while in captivity wrote "The Essence of Russian History." The book was finished in 1715 and published in 1770. Both of these works were imbued with patriotism, and gave a rational explanation of historical events and developments. In 1720 a leading Russian historian of the nobility, V. N. Tatishchev, started working on his History of Russia. A renowned diplomat, B. I. Kurakin, wrote a "History of Tsar Peter Alekseevich."

On January 28, 1724, an ukaz was signed founding the Academy of Sciences, which was opened in 1725. At the Academy was a University and a Gymnasium to train educated people qualified to do scientific work. . . .

In 1702 in Moscow, and later in Petersburg, were opened public theaters ("comedy temples"), where plays of exclusively secular nature were performed (among historical subjects—Alexander the Great, Julius Caesar, "A Comedy about Don Juan and Don Pedro," comedies by Molière, "Amphitryon," "L'Amour médecin," and others). At the Moscow theater was a school for actors consisting of young Russian officials. For spectacles in Petrograd, troupes and individual artists from Western European countries were invited. The interest in drama led to the appearance of "independent" theaters at various schools and at Moscow Hospital. There appeared the first dramas written by Russians about Russian subjects. . . .

Elements of realism penetrated gradually into literature. The works of the time reflected diverse aspects of the life of nobles and merchants ("Story About a Russian Seaman Vasilii Koriotskii"; "Story About a Russian Nobleman Named Alexander"; "A Story About Frol Skobeev"; "A Story About a Russian Merchant Named Ivan"; and others). Love, lyric, and secular poetry were also disseminated (as for example an ode about the Battle of Poltava by F. Prokopovich). . . .

Life gradually altered the routine tenor of living and introduced into it new novelties. Already in the seventeenth century, among the upper classes of society a taste for "Polish" clothes, "shaving," and "smoking" developed. These innovations were criticized by the defenders of the status quo. In Peter's view, the beard and long apparel were symbols of boiar arrogance and conceit, laziness, and clumsiness. Peter allowed wearing of beards for the clergy, city dwellers, and peasants, but personally cut off the beards and the long clothes of the boiars. Nobles who served in the army or the fleet were ordered to wear a uniform with a sign of distinction and an appropriate cut. It was decreed to salute not in accordance with the old boiar pattern or a noble title, but according to a rank based on the "Table of Ranks."

The new order of things imposed its imprint on the pattern of life and habits of nobles and merchants and on their family life. The patriarchal pattern with its purely religious outlook gave way to secular life, to rationalism, and to a businesslike pattern.

The outlook of social interests was also broadened. To satisfy some of the new needs meetings of nobles in private homes were officially inaugurated. For the social guidance of young nobles, there was published a book translated from the German entitled "An Honest Mirror for the Young"; as an example for business and domestic correspondence, there was published a book entitled "Examples of How to Write Various Compliments."

Serious achievements in the development of science, literature, and art in the first quarter of the eighteenth century were a major phase in the history of Russian national culture. Simultaneously, cultural changes reflected clearly class character, and supported the needs of the dominant exploiting classes. Russian nobles and merchants began to read widely; became acquainted with the culture, life, and customs of western countries. A number of achievements borrowed from western culture (especially those in the natural sciences, technology, scientific terminology, etc.) had a positive significance. But the superfluous fascination with forms alien to the way of life of the Russian people, the littering of the Russian national language with foreign words and meanings adopted without any discrimination laid the foundation for servility before everything foreign. This phenomenon became widespread among a good portion of Russian nobles in subsequent decades.

PART II

Modernization of Russia Under Catherine II

1   *Catherine II's Instruction:*
Modernization Through Plagiarism

Catherine II (1762–1796) was one of the most enlightened despots of eighteenth-century Europe. As Russia's empress she tried to bring to a successful conclusion the work of modernization that had been started by Peter I. During her reign, the city of St. Petersburg emerged as a major cultural center of Europe, and many intellectual giants of the French Enlightenment saw in her the embodiment of "Reason." Under the influence of their ideas she composed the Nakaz, *or* Instruction *to the Legislative Commission of 1767–1768. This document, which Voltaire called the finest monument of the century, reflected Catherine's ambition to remodel Russia's laws, institutions, and society in accordance with the new principles being expounded in Western Europe.*

"O Lord my God, hearken unto me, and instruct me; that I may administer Judgment unto thy People; as thy sacred Laws direct to judge with Righteousness!"

SOURCE. *The Grand Instruction to the Commissioners Appointed to Frame a New Code of Laws for the Russian Empire. Composed by Her Imperial Majesty Catherine II* . . . Translated by Michael Tatischeff (London: 1768), pp. 69–79, 80–82, 85–90, 95–97, 104–106, 115–118, 126–128, 132–141, 159–166, 178–181, and 194–196. Spelling of some words has been modernized to facilitate reading.

THE INSTRUCTIONS TO THE COMMISSIONERS
FOR COMPOSING A NEW CODE OF LAWS

1. The Christian Law teaches us to do mutual Good to one another, as much as possibly we can.

2. Laying this down as a fundamental Rule prescribed by that Religion, which has taken, or ought to take Root in the Hearts of the whole People; we cannot but suppose that every honest Man in the Community is, or will be, desirous of seeing his native Country at the very summit of Happiness, Glory, Safety, and Tranquillity.

3. And that every Individual Citizen in particular must wish to see himself protected by Laws, which should not distress him in his Circumstances, but, on the Contrary, should defend him from all Attempts of others that are repugnant to this fundamental Rule.

4. In order therefore to proceed to a speedy Execution of what We expect from such a general Wish, We, fixing the Foundation upon the above first-mentioned Rule, ought to begin with an Inquiry into the natural Situation of this Empire.

5. For those Laws have the greatest Conformity with Nature, whose particular Regulations are best adapted to the Situation and Circumstances of the Pople for whom they are instituted.

This natural Situation is described in the three following Chapters.

CHAPTER I

6. Russia is an European State.

7. This is clearly demonstrated by the following Observations: The Alterations which *Peter the Great* undertook in Russia succeeded with the greater Ease, because the Manners, which prevailed at that Time, and had been introduced amongst us by a Mixture of different Nations, and the Conquest of foreign Territories, were quite unsuitable to the Climate. *Peter the First,* by introducing the Manners and Customs of Europe among the European People in his Dominions, found at that Time such Means as even he himself was not sanguine enough to expect.

CHAPTER II

8. The Possessions of the Russian Empire extend upon the terrestrial Globe to 32 Degrees of Latitude, and to 165 of Longitude.

9. The Sovereign is absolute; for there is no other authority but that which centers in his single Person that can act with a Vigour proportionate to the Extent of such a vast Dominion.

10. The Extent of the Dominion requires an absolute Power to be vested in that Person who rules over it. It is expedient so to be that the quick Dispatch of Affairs, sent from distant Parts, might make ample Amends for the Delay occasioned by the great Distance of the Places.

11. Every other Form of Government whatsoever would not only have been prejudicial to Russia, but would even have proved its entire Ruin.

12. Another Reason is; That it is better to be subject to the Laws under one Master, than to be subservient to many.

13. What is the true End of Monarchy? Not to deprive People of their natural Liberty; but to correct their Actions, in order to attain the *supreme* Good.

14. The Form of Government, therefore, which best attains this End, and at the same Time sets less Bounds than others to natural Liberty, is that which coincides with the Views and Purposes of rational Creatures, and answers the End, upon which we ought to fix a stedfast Eye in the Regulations of civil Polity.

15. The Intention and the End of Monarchy is the Glory of the Citizens, of the State, and of the Sovereign.

16. But, from this Glory, a Sense of Liberty arises in a People governed by a Monarch; which may produce in these States as much Energy in transacting the most important Affairs, and may contribute as much to the Happiness of the Subjects, as even Liberty itself.

CHAPTER III

17. *Of the Safety of the Institutions of Monarchy.*

18. The intermediate Powers, subordinate to, and depending

upon the supreme Power, form the essential Part of monarchical Government.

19. *I* have said, that the intermediate Powers, subordinate and depending, proceed from the supreme Power; as in the very Nature of the Thing the Sovereign is the Souce of all imperial and civil Power.

20. The Laws, which form the Foundation of the State, send out certain Courts of Judicature, through which, as through smaller Streams, the Power of the Government is poured out, and diffused.

21. The Laws allow these Courts of Judicature to remonstrate, that such or such an Injunction is unconstitutional, and prejudicial, obscure, and impossible to be carried into Execution; and direct, beforehand, to which Injunction one ought to pay Obedience, and in what Manner one ought to conform to it. These Laws undoubtedly constitute the firm and immovable Basis of every State.

CHAPTER IV

22. There must be a political Body, to whom the Care and strict Execution of these Laws ought to be confided.

23. This Care, and strict Execution of the Laws, can be no where so properly fixed as in certain Courts of Judicature, which announce to the People the newly-made Laws, and revive those which are forgotten, or obsolete.

24. And it is the Duty of these Courts of Judicature to examine carefully those Laws which they receive from the Sovereign, and to remonstrate, if they find any Thing in them repugnant to the fundamental Constitution of the State, etc., which has been already remarked above in the third Chapter, and twenty-first Article.

25. But if they find nothing in them of that Nature, they enter them in the Code of Laws already established in the State, and publish them to the whole Body of the People.

26. In Russia the Senate is the political Body, to which the Care and due Execution of the Laws is confided.

27. All other Courts of Judicature may, and ought to remon-

strate with the same Propriety, to the State, and even to the Sovereign himself, as was already mentioned above.

28. Should any One inquire, wherein the Care and due Execution of the Laws consists? I answer That the Care and due Execution of the Laws produces particular Instructions; in consequence of which the before-mentioned Courts of Judicature, instituted to the End that, by their Care, the Will of the Sovereign might be obeyed in a Manner conformably to the fundamental Laws and Constitution of the State, are obliged to act, in the Discharge of their Duty, according to the Rules prescribed.

29. These Instructions will prevent the People from transgressing the Injunctions of the Sovereign with impunity; but, at the same Time, will protect them from the Insults and ungovernable Passions of others.

30. For, on the one Hand, they justify the Penalties prepared for those who transgress the Laws; and, on the other, they confirm the Justice of that Refusal to enter Laws repugnant to the good Order of the State, amongst those which are already approved of, or to act by those Laws in the Administration of Justice, and the general Business of the Whole Body of the People.

CHAPTER V

31. *Of the Situation of the People in general.*

32. It is the greatest Happiness for a Man to be so circumstanced, that, if his Passions should prompt him to be mischievous, he should still think it more for his Interest not to give Way to them.

33. The Laws ought to be so framed as to secure the Safety of every Citizen as much as possible.

34. The Equality of the Citizens consists in this; that they should all be subject to the same Laws.

35. This Equality requires Institutions so well adapted as to prevent the Rich from oppressing those who are not so wealthy as themselves, and converting all the Charges and Employments intrusted to them as Magistrates only to their own private Emolument.

36. General or political Liberty does not consist in that licentious Notion, *That a Man may do whatever he pleases.*

37. In a State or Assemblage of People that live together in a Community, where there are Laws, Liberty can only consist *in doing that which every One ought to do,* and *not to be constrained to do that which One ought not to do.*

38. A Man ought to form in his own Mind an exact and clear Idea of what Liberty is. *Liberty is the Right of doing whatsoever the Laws allow:* And if any one Citizen could do what the Laws forbid, there would be no more Liberty; because others would have an equal Power of doing the same.

39. The political Liberty of a Citizen is the Peace of Mind arising from the Consciousness that every Individual enjoys his peculiar Safety; and in order that the People might attain this Liberty, the Laws ought to be so framed that no one Citizen should stand in Fear of another; but that all of them should stand in Fear of the same Laws.

CHAPTER VI

40. *Of Laws in general.*

41. Nothing ought to be forbidden by the Laws but what may be prejudicial, either to every Individual in particular, or to the whole Community in general.

42. All Actions which comprehend nothing of this Nature are in nowise cognizable by the Laws; which are made only with the View of procuring the greatest possible Advantage and Tranquillity to the People, who live under their Protection.

43. To preserve Laws from being violated, they ought to be so good, and so well furnished with all Expedients, tending to procure the greatest possible Good to the People; that every Individual might be fully convinced that it was his Interest, as well as Duty, to preserve those Laws inviolable.

44. And this is the most exalted Pitch of Perfection which we ought to labour to attain to.

45. Many Things rule over Mankind. Religion, the Climate, Laws, the Maxims received from Government, the Example of past Ages, Manners, and Customs. . . .

56. By what *I* have here advanced, *I* meant not, in the least, to abridge that infinite Distance which must ever subsist between

Vices and Virtues. God forbid! *My* Intention was only to show that all the *political* Vices are not moral Vices; and that all the *moral* Vices are not *political* Ones. This Distinction ought to be known and carefully attended to, that in making the Laws nothing may be introduced in them which is contrary to the general Sense of a Nation.

57. The Legislation ought to adapt its Laws to the general Sense of a Nation. We do nothing so well as what we do freely and uncontrolled, and following the natural Bent of our own Inclinations.

58. In order to introduce better Laws, it is essentially necessary to prepare the Minds of the People for their Reception. But that it may never be pleaded in Excuse that it is impossible to carry even the most useful Affairs into Execution because the Minds of the People are not yet prepared for it, you must, in that Case, take the Trouble upon yourselves to prepare them; and, by these Means, you will already have done a great Part of the Work.

59. Laws are the peculiar and distinct Institutions of the Legislator; but Manners and Customs are the Institutions of the whole Body of the People.

60. Consequently, if there should be a Necessity of making great Alterations amongst the People for their greater Benefit: that must be corrected by Laws which has been instituted by Laws, and that must be amended by Custom which has been introduced by Custom; and it is extreme bad Policy to alter that by Laws which ought to be altered by Custom.

61. There are means of preventing the Growth of Crimes, and these are the Punishments inflicted by the Laws. At the same Time there are Means for introducing an Alteration in Customs, and these are Examples.

62. Besides, the more a People have an Intercourse with one another, the more easy it is for them to introduce a Change in their Customs.

63. In a Word, every Punishment which is not inflicted through Necessity, is tyrannical. The Law has not its Source merely from Power. Things indifferent in their Nature do not come under the Cognizance of the Laws.

CHAPTER VII

64. *Of the Laws in particular.*

65. Laws carried to the Extremity of Right are productive of the Extremity of Evil.

66. All laws, where the Legislation aims at the Extremity of Rigour, may be evaded. It is Moderation which rules a People, and not Excess of Severity.

67. Civil Liberty flourishes when the Laws deduce every Punishment from the peculiar Nature of every Crime. The Application of Punishment ought not to proceed from the arbitrary Will, or mere Caprice of the Legislator, but from the Nature of the Crime; and it is not the Man, who ought to do Violence to a Man, but the proper Action of the Man himself. . . .

CHAPTER VIII

80. *Of Punishments.*

81. The Love of our Country, Shame, and the Dread of public Censure, are Motives which restrain, and may deter Mankind from the Commission of a Number of Crimes.

82. The greatest Punishment for a bad Action, under a mild Administration, will be for the Party to be convinced of it. The civil Laws will there correct Vice with the more Ease, and will not be under a Necessity of employing more rigorous Means.

83. In these Governments, the Legislature will apply itself more to prevent Crimes than to punish them, and should take more Care to instil Good Manners into the Minds of the Citizens, by proper Regulations, than to dispirit them by the Terror of corporal and capital Punishments.

84. In a Word, whatever is termed Punishment in the Law is, in Fact, nothing but Pain and Suffering.

85. Experience teaches us that, in those Countries where Punishments are mild, they operate with the same Efficacy upon the Minds of the Citizens as the most severe in other Places.

86. If a sensible Injury should accrue to a State from some popular Commotion, a violent Administration will be at once for a sudden Remedy, and instead of recurring to the ancient Laws,

will inflict some terrible Punishment, in order to crush the growing Evil on the Spot. The Imagination of the People is affected at the Time of this Greater Punishment, just as it would have been affected by the least; and when the Dread of this Punishment gradually wears off, it will be compelled to introduce a severer Punishment upon all Occasions.

87. The People ought not to be driven on by violent Methods, but we ought to make Use of the Means which Nature has given us, with the utmost Care and Caution, in order to conduct them to the End we propose.

88. Examine with Attention the Cause of all Licentiousness; and you will find that it proceeds from the Neglect of punishing Crimes, not from the Mildness of Punishments. Let us follow Nature, which has given Shame to Man for his Scourge and let the greatest Part of the Punishment consist in the Infamy which accompanies the Punishment.

89. And if a Country could be found where Infamy should not be the Consequence of Punishment; the Reason of this is to be imputed to some tyrannical Government, which inflicted the same Punishments upon the Innocent and the Guilty, without Distinction.

90. And if another Country should be known where the People are restrained by nothing but the severest Punishments; you must again be assured that this proceeds from the Violence of the Government, which has ordained those Punishments for the slightest Offences.

91. It happens frequently that a Legislator, who wants to extirpate an Evil, thinks of nothing but this Method of Cure: His Eyes are fixed on this Object only, and do not foresee the bad Consequences which attend it. When the Evil is once cured, we remark nothing but the Severity of the Legislator; but it leaves a Distemper in the State, arising from this very Severity. The Minds of the People are corrupted, for they are inured to Despotism. . . .

94. It is unjust to punish a Thief who robs on the Highway in the same Manner as another, who not only robs, but commits Murder. Every One sees clearly that some Difference ought to be made in their Punishment, for the Sake of the general Safety. . . .

96. Good Laws keep strictly a just Medium: They do not always inflict pecuniary, nor always subject Malefactors to corporal Punishment.

All Punishments by which the human Body might be maimed ought to be abolished.

CHAPTER IX

97. *Of the Administration of Justice in general.* . . .

119. The Laws which condemn a Man upon the Deposition of one Evidence only are destructive to Liberty. . . .

120. Two Witnesses are absolutely necessary in order to form a right Judgment: For an Accuser, who affirms, and the Party accused, who denies the Fact, make the Evidence on both Sides equal; for that Reason, a Third is required in order to convict the Defendant; unless other clear collateral Proofs should fix the Credibility of the Evidence in favour of one of them.

121. The Evidence of two Witnesses is esteemed sufficient for Conviction in every criminal Case whatsoever. The Law believes them, as if they spoke from the Mouth of Truth itself. . . .

123. The Usage of Torture is contrary to all the Dictates of Nature and Reason; even Mankind itself cries out against it, and demands loudly the total Abolition of it. We see, at this very Time, a People greatly renowned for the Excellence of their civil Polity, who reject it without any sensible Inconveniencies. It is, therefore, by no Means necessary by its Nature. We will explain this more at large here below.

124. There are Laws which do not allow the Application of Torture, except only in those Cases where the Prisoner at the Bar refuses to plead, and will neither acknowledge himself innocent nor guilty.

125. To make an Oath too cheap by frequent Practice is to weaken the Obligation of it, and to destroy its Efficacy. The Kissing of the Cross cannot be used upon any Occasion, but when he that takes an Oath has no private Interest of his own to serve; as for Instance, the Judge and the Witnesses.

126. Those who are to be tried for capital Offences should choose their own Judges, with the Consent of the Laws; or, at

least, should have a Right of rejecting such a Number of them that those who remain in Court may seem as chosen by the Malefactors themselves.

127. It is likewise just that some of the Judges should be of the same Rank of Citizenship as the Defendant; that is, his Equals; that he might not think himself fallen into the Hands of such People as would violently over-rule the Affair to his Prejudice: Of this there are already Instances in the Martial Laws.

128. When the Defendant is condemned, it is not the Judges who inflict the Punishment upon him, but the Law.

129. The Sentence ought to be as clear and distinct as possible; even so far as to preserve the very identical Words of the Law. But if they should include the private Opinion of the Judge, the People will live in Society without knowing exactly the reciprocal Obligations they lie under to one another in that State. . . .

153. Nothing is so dangerous as this general Axiom: *The Spirit of the Law ought to be considered, and not the Letter.* This can mean nothing else but to break down the Fence which opposes the Torrent of popular Opinions. This is a self-evident Truth which is not to be controverted, how strange soever it may appear to vulgar Minds; who are more terrified by the least Irregularity which happens before their Eyes than by Consequences more remote, but infinitely more fatal, which flow from one false Principle adopted by a People. Every Man has his own particular Mode of viewing Objects presented to his Mind, different from every other. We should see the Fate of a Citizen changed, by the Removal of his Cause from one Court of Judicature to another; and his Life and Liberty depending upon Chance, either from some false Ideas, or the Perverseness of his Judge: We should see the *same* Crimes punished *differently,* at *different* Times, by the *very same* Court of Judicature; if they will not listen to the invariable Voice of the fixed, established Laws, but follow the deceitful Inconstancy of their own arbitrary Interpretations.

154. The Disorders which may possibly arise from a *strict* and *close* Adherence to *the Letter* of *penal* Laws, are by no Means comparable to those which are produced by the *arbitrary Interpretation* of them. The Errors proceeding from the *first* are

only *temporary*, and will oblige the Legislator to make, some-times, easy and necessary Corrections in such *Words* of the Law as are capable of a *double Meaning*. However, it will prove a Bridle to curb that *licentious* Method of *interpreting* and *decid-ing* at *their own Discretion*, which may prove fatal to every citi-zen.

155. If the Laws are not *exactly* and *clearly* defined, and un-derstood *Word by Word;* if it be not the sole Office of a Judge to *distinguish* and lay down *clearly*, what Action is conformable to the Laws, and what is repugnant to them: If the Rule of *just* and *unjust*, which ought to govern alike the ignorant Clown and the enlightened Scholar, be not a *simple Question* of Matter of Fact for the Judges; then the Situation of the Citizen will be exposed to strange Accidents.

156. By making the *penal* Laws always *clearly* intelligible, *Word by Word*, every one may calculate truly and know exactly the Inconveniences of a bad Action; a Knowledge which is *abso-lutely* necessary for restraining People from committing it; and the People may enjoy Security with respect both to their Persons and Property; which ought ever to remain so, because this is the *main Scope* and *Object* of the Laws, and without which the Community would be dissolved.

157. If the Power of *interpreting* Laws be an Evil, there is an Evil also which attends the *Obscurity* of them, and lays us under the Necessity of having Recourse to their Interpretation. This Ir-regularity is still greater when the Laws are written in a Lan-guage *unknown* to the People, or expressed in *uncommon* Phrases.

158. The Laws ought to be written in the *common vernacular Tongue*; and the Code, which contains all the Laws, ought to be esteemed as a Book of the utmost Use, which should be pur-chased at as *small* a Price as the Catechism. If the Case were otherwise, and the Citizen should be ignorant of the Conse-quences of his own Actions, and what concerns his Person and Liberty, he will then depend upon some few of the People who have taken upon themselves the Care of preserving and explain-ing them. Crimes will be less frequent in *proportion* as the Code of Laws is more *universally* read, and *comprehended* by the Peo-ple. And, for this Reason, it must be ordained, That, in all the Schools, Children should be taught to read *alternately* out of the

Church Books and out of *those* which contain the Laws. . . .

193. The Torture of the Rack is a Cruelty established and made use of by many Nations, and is applied to the Party accused during the Course of his Trial, either to extort from him a Confession of his Guilt, or in order to clear up some Contradictions in which he had involved himself during his Examination, or to compel him to discover his Accomplices, or in order to discover other Crimes, of which, though he is not accused, yet he may *perhaps* be guilty.

194. (1) No Man ought to be looked upon as *guilty* before he has received his judicial Sentence; nor can the Laws deprive him of *their* Protection before it is proved that he has *forfeited all Right* to it. What Right therefore can Power give to any to inflict Punishment upon a Citizen at a Time when it is yet dubious whether he is *innocent* or *guilty?* Whether the Crime be known or unknown, it is not very difficult to gain a thorough Knowledge of the Affair by duly weighing all the Circumstances. If the Crime be known, the Criminal ought not to suffer any Punishment but what the Law ordains; consequently the Rack is quite unnecessary. If the Crime be not known, the Rack ought not to be applied to the Party accused; for this Reason, *That the Innocent ought not to be tortured;* and, in the Eye of the Law, every Person is innocent whose Crime is not yet *proved.* It is undoubtedly extremely necessary that no Crime, after it has been proved, should remain unpunished. The Party accused on the Rack, whilst in the Agonies of Torture, is not Master enough of himself to be able to declare the Truth. Can we give more Credit to a Man when he is light-headed in a Fever, than when he enjoys the free Use of his Reason in a State of Health? The Sensation of Pain may arise to such a Height that, after having subdued the whole Soul, it will leave her no longer the Liberty of producing any proper Act of the Will, except that of taking the shortest instantaneous Method, in the very twinkling of an Eye, as it were, of getting rid of her Torment. In such an Extremity, even an *innocent* Person will roar out that he is *guilty*, only to gain *some Respite* from his Tortures. Thus the very same Expedient, which is made use of to distinguish the *Innocent* from the *Guilty*, will take away the *whole Difference* between them; and the Judges will be as uncertain whether they have an *innocent* or a *guilty*

Person before them, as they were before the Beginning of this *partial* Way of Examination. The Rack, therefore, is a sure Method of condemning an innocent Person of a weakly Constitution, and of acquitting a *wicked Wretch*, who depends upon the Robustness of his Frame.

195. (2) The Rack is likewise made use of to oblige the Party accused to clear up (as they term it) the Contradictions in which he has involved himself in the Course of his Examination; as if the Dread of Punishment, the Uncertainty and Anxiety in determining what to way, and even gross Ignorance itself, common to both *Innocent and Guilty, could not lead a timorous Innocent,* and a *Delinquent* who seeks to hide his Villanies, into Contradictions; and as if Contradictions, which are so common to Man even in a State of Ease and Tranquillity, would not increase in that Perturbation of Soul, when he is plunged entirely in Reflections of how to escape the Danger he is threatened with.

196. (3) To make use of the Rack for discovering whether the Party accused has not committed *other* Crimes, besides *that* which he has been *convicted of,* is a certain Expedient to *screen every Crime* from its *proper* Punishment: For a Judge will always be discovering new Ones. Finally, this Method of Proceeding will be founded upon the following Way of reasoning: *Thou art guilty of one Crime, therefore, perhaps, thou hast committed an Hundred others: According to the Laws, thou wilt be tortured and tormented; not only because thou art guilty, but even because thou mayest be still more guilty.*

197. (4) Besides this, the Party accused is tortured, to oblige him to discover his Accomplices. But when we have already proved that the Rack cannot be the proper Means for searching out the Truth, then how can it give any assistance in discovering the Accomplices in a Crime? It is undoubtedly extremely easy for him, who accuses himself, to accuse others. Besides, is it just to torture one Man for the Crimes of others? Might not the Accomplices be discovered by examining the Witnesses who were produced against the Criminal, by a strict Inquiry into the Proofs alleged against him, and even by the Nature of the Fact itself, and the Circumstances which happened at the Time when the Crime was committed? In short, by all the Means which serve to prove the Delinquent guilty of the Crime he had committed? . . . .

220. A Punishment ought to be *immediate, analogous* to the *Nature* of the Crime, and *known* to the Public.

221. The *sooner* the Punishment succeeds to the Commission of a Crime, the more *useful* and *just* it will be. *Just;* because it will spare the Malefactor the torturing and useless Anguish of Heart about the *Uncertainty* of his Destiny. Consequently the Decision of an Affair, in a Court of Judicature, ought to be finished in as little Time as possible. *I have said before that Punishment immediately inflicted is most useful;* the Reason is because the smaller the Interval of Time is which passes between the Crime and the Punishment, the *more* the Crime will be esteemed as a *Motive* to the Punishment, and the Punishment as an *Effect* of the Crime. Punishment must be *certain* and *unavoidable.*

222. The most certain Curb upon Crimes is not the *Severity* of the Punishment, but the absolute Conviction in the People that Delinquents will be *inevitably* punished.

223. The *Certainty* even of a small, but *inevitable* Punishment, will make a *stronger* Impression on the Mind than the *Dread* even of *capital* Punishment, connected with the Hopes of escaping it. As Punishments become *more* mild and moderate; Mercy and Pardon will be less necessary in Proportion, for the Laws themselves, at such a time, are replete with the *Spirit* of Mercy.

224. However extensive a State may be, *every Part* of it must depend upon the Laws.

225. We must endeavour to exterminate Crimes in general, *particularly* those which are *most* injurious to the Community: Consequently, the Means made use of by the Laws to deter People from the Commission of every Kind of Crimes ought to be the *most* powerful, in proportion as the Crimes are *more* destructive to the Public Good, and in proportion to the *Strength* of the Temptation by which *weak* or *bad* Minds may be *allured* to the Commission of them. Consequently, there ought to be a *fixed* stated Proportion between *Crimes* and *Punishments.*

226. If there be two Crimes, which injure the Community *unequally,* and yet receive *equal* Punishment; then the *unequal* Distribution of the Punishment will produce this *strange Contradiction,* very little *noticed* by any one, thought it frequently happens, that the *Laws* will punish Crimes which *proceed* from *the Laws themselves.*

227. If the *same* Punishment should be inflicted upon a Man for killing an *Animal* as for killing *another Man,* or for *Forgery,* the People will soon make no *Difference* between *those Crimes.* . . .

239. (Q. 8) *Which are the most efficacious Means of preventing Crimes?*

240. It is better to *prevent* Crimes than to *punish* them.

241. To *prevent* Crimes is the *Intention* and the *End* of every good Legislation; which is nothing more than the Art of conducting People to the *greatest* Good, or to leave the *least* Evil possible amongst them, if it should prove impracticable to *exterminate* the whole.

242. If we forbid many Actions which are termed *indifferent* by the *Moralists,* we shall not prevent the Crimes of which they *may* be productive, but shall *create* still *new* Ones.

243. Would you *prevent* Crimes? order it so, That the Laws might rather favour every *Individual,* than any particular Rank of Citizens, in the Community.

244. Order it so, that the People should fear *the Laws,* and *nothing* but the Laws.

245. Would you prevent Crimes? order it so, that the *Light of Knowledge* may be *diffused* among the People.

246. A Book of good Laws is nothing but a Bar to prevent the Licentiousness of injurious Men from doing Mischief to their fellow Creatures.

247. There is yet another Expedient to *prevent* Crimes, which is by *rewarding* Virtue.

248. Finally, the *most sure* but, at the same Time, the *most difficult* Expedient to mend the Morals of the People, is a perfect System of Education. . . .

CHAPTER XI

250. A Society of Citizens, as well as every Thing else, requires a certain fixed Order: There ought to be *some to govern,* and *others to obey.*

251. And this is the Origin of every Kind of Subjection; which feels itself more or less alleviated, in Proportion to the Situation of the Subjects.

252. And, consequently, as the Law of Nature commands *Us* to take as much Care as lies in *Our* Power of the Prosperity of all the People; we are obliged to alleviate the Situation of the Subjects as much as sound Reason will permit.

253. And therefore, to shun all Occasions of reducing People to a State of Slavery, except that the *utmost* Necessity should *inevitably* oblige us to do it; in that Case, it ought not to be done for our own Benefit; but for the Interest of the State: Yet even that Case is extremely uncommon.

254. Of whatever Kind Subjection may be, the civil Laws ought to guard, on the one Hand, against the *Abuse* of Slavery, and, on the other, against the *Dangers* which may arise from it.

255. Unhappy is that Government which is compelled to institute *severe* Laws.

256. *Peter the Great* ordained, in the Year 1722, that Persons who were insane in Mind, and those who tortured their Vassals, should be put under the Tutelage of Guardians. This Injunction is executed with regard to the Objects of the first Part of it; the Reason why it is not put in Force with respect to the Objects of the last Part is *unknown*. . . .

260. A great Number of Slaves ought not to be infranchised all at once, nor by a general Law.

261. A Law may be productive of public Benefit, which gives some *private* Property to a Slave.

262. Let us finish all this, by repeating that *fundamental Rule;* that the government which most resembles that of Nature is that whose particular Disposition answers best to the Disposition of the People, for whom it is instituted.

263. However it is still highly necessary to prevent those Causes which so frequently incited Slaves to rebel against their masters; but till these Causes are discovered, it is impossible to prevent the like accidents by Laws; though the Tranquillity, both of the one and of the other, depends upon it. . . .

CHAPTER XIII

293. *Of handicraft Trades, and Commerce.*

294. There can be neither skillful Handicraftsmen, nor a firm-

ly-established Commerce, where Agriculture is neglected, or carried on with Supineness and Negligence.

295. Agriculture can never flourish there, where no Persons have any property of their own.

296. This is founded upon a very simple Rule: *Every Man will take more Care of his own Property, than of that which belongs to another; and will not exert his utmost Endeavours upon that which he has Reason to fear another may deprive him of.*

297. Agriculture is the most laborious Employment a Man can undertake. The *more* the Climate induces a Man to shun this Trouble, the *more* the Laws ought to animate him to it. . . .

299. It would not be improper to give a Premium to those Husbandmen who bring their Fields into better Order than others.

300. And to the Handicraftsmen, who distinguished themselves most by their Care and Skill.

301. This Regulation will produce a Progress in the Arts, in all Parts of the Country. It was of Service, even in our own Times, in establishing very important Manufactories.

302. There are Countries where a Treatise of Agriculture, published by the Government, is lodged in every Church, from which the Peasant may be able to get the better of his Difficulties, and draw proper Advantage from the Instructions it contains.

303. There are Nations inclined to Laziness. In order to exterminate Laziness in the Inhabitants, arising from the Climate, such Laws are to be made as should deprive those who refuse to work, of the Means of Subsistence.

304. All Nations inclined to Laziness are arrogant in their Behaviour; for they who do not work esteem themselves, in some Measure, Rulers over those who labour.

305. Nations who have given themselves up to Idleness are generally proud: We might turn the Effect against the Cause from which it proceeds, and destroy Laziness by Pride itself.

306. For Government may be as strongly supported by *Ambition* as it may be endangered by *Pride.* In asserting this, we need only represent to ourselves, on the one hand, the innumerable Benefits which result from *Ambition;* such as, Industry, Arts, and Sciences, Politeness, Taste, etc., and on the other, the infi-

nite Number of Evils arising from *Pride*, in some Nations; such as Laziness, Poverty, Disregard for every thing; the Destruction of Nations, who accidentally fall into their Power, and afterwards the Ruin of themselves.

307. As *Pride* induces some to shun Labour, so *Ambition* impels others to excel all the rest in Workmanship.

308. View every Nation with Attention, and you will find that arrogant Pride and Laziness, most commonly, go Hand in Hand together. . . .

311. A Man is not poor because he has nothing; but because he will do no Work. He who has no Estate, but will work, may live as well as he, who has an annual Income of a Hundred Rubles, but will do no Work.

312. A Tradesman who has taught his Children his Art, has given them such an Estate as increases in proportion to their Number.

313. Agriculture is the first and principal Labour which ought to be encouraged in the People: The next is the manufacturing our own Produce.

314. Machines, which serve to shorten Labour in the mechanic Arts, are not always useful. If a Piece of Work, wrought with the Hands, can be afforded at a Price equally advantageous to the Merchant and the Manufacturer; in this Case, Machines which shorten Labour, that is, which diminish the Number of Workmen, will be greatly prejudicial to a populous Country.

315. Yet, we ought to distinguish between what we manufacture for our Home-consumption, and what we manufacture for Exportation into foreign Countries.

316. Too much Use cannot be made of this Kind of Machines in our Manufactures, which we export to other Nations; who do, or may receive the same Kind of Goods, from our Neighbours or other People; especially those who are in the same Situation with ourselves.

317. Commerce flies from Places where it meets with Oppression, and settles where it meets with Protection. . . .

319. In many Countries, where all the Taxes are farmed, the *Collection* of the Royal Revenues *ruins* Commerce, not only by its Inequality, Oppression, and extreme Exactions, but also by the Difficulties it occasions, and the Formalities it requires.

320. In other Places, where the Duties or Customs are *collected* upon the *good Faith* of the Importers, there is a wide Difference in respect of the Conveniencies for Traffick. One Word in Writing transacts the greatest Business. The Merchant is under no Necessity of losing Time in Attendance; nor obliged to employ *Clerks*, on purpose to remove the Difficulties started by the *Financiers*, or be *compelled* to submit to them.

321. The Liberty of Trading does not consist in a Permission to Merchants of doing whatever they please; this would be rather the *Slavery* of Commerce: What *cramps* the Trader does not *cramp* the Trade. In free Countries the Merchant meets with innumerable Obstacles; but in despotic Governments he is not near so much thwarted by the Laws. England prohibits the Exportation of its Wool; she has ordained Coals to be imported to the Capital by Sea; she has prohibited the Exportation of Horses fit for Stallions; she obliges Ships, which Trade from her Plantations in America into Europe, to anchor first in England. By these, and such like Prohibitions, she *cramps* the Merchant; but it is for the *Benefit* of Commerce.

322. Wherever there is Trade, there are Custom-houses also.

323. The Object of Trade is the Exportation and Importation of Goods, for the Advantage of the State: The Object of the Custom-houses is a certain Duty, exacted from the same Exportation and Importation of Goods, for the Advantage likewise of the State; for this Reason a State ought to preserve an exact Impartiality between the Custom-house and the Trade, and to make such proper Regulations that these two might never clash with each other: Then the People will enjoy there free Liberty of Commerce. . . .

CHAPTER XIV

347. *Of Education.*

348. The Rules of Education are the fundamental Institutes which train us up to be Citizens.

349. Each particular Family ought to be governed upon the Plan of the great Family; which includes all the Particulars.

350. It is impossible to give a general Education to a very nu-

merous People, and to bring up all the Children in Houses regulated for that Purpose; and, for that Reason, it will be proper to establish some *general Rules,* which may serve by *Way of Advice* to all Parents.

351. Every Parent is obliged to teach his Children the Fear of God as the Beginning of all Wisdom, and to inculcate into them all those Duties, which God demands from us in the ten Commandments, and our orthodox Eastern Greek Religion, in its Rules and Traditions.

352. Also to inculcate into them the Love of their Country, and to enure them to pay due Respect to the established civil Laws, and to reverence the Courts of Judicature in their Country, as those who, by the Appointment of God, watch over their Happiness in this World.

353. Every Parent ought to refrain *in Presence* of his Children, not only from *Actions,* but even *Words* that tend to Injustice and Violence; as for Instance, *Quarrelling, Swearing, Fighting, every Sort of Cruelty,* and *such like Behaviour;* and not to allow those who are about his Children *to set them such bad Examples.*

354. He ought to forbid his Children, and those who are about them, the *Vice of lying,* though even *in jest;* for *Lying* is the most pernicious of *all Vices.*

355. We shall add here, for the Instruction of every Man in particular, what has been already printed, and serves as a *general Rule* for the Schools already founded, and which are still founding by *Us,* for *Education,* and for the *whole Society.*

356. *Every one ought to inculcate the Fear of God into the tender Minds of Children, to encourage every laudable Inclination, and to accustom them to the fundamental Rules, suitable to their respective Situations; to incite in them a Desire for Labour, and a Dread of Idleness, as the Root of all Evil, and Error; to train them up to a proper Decorum in their Actions and Conversation, Civility, and Decency in their Behaviour; and to sympathise with the Miseries of poor unhappy Wretches; and to break them of all perverse and forward Humours; to teach them Economy, and whatever is most useful in all Affairs of Life; to guard them against all Prodigality and Extravagance; and particularly to root a proper Love of Cleanliness and Neatness, as well in*

themselves as in those who belong to them; in a Word, to instill all those Virtues and Qualities which join to form a good Education; by which, as they grow up, they may prove real Citizens, useful Members of the Community, and Ornaments to their Country....

CONCLUSION

523. *Perhaps some Persons may object, after perusing these Instructions, that they will not be intelligible to every one. To this it may be answered: It is true, they will not be readily understood by every Person after one slight Perusal only; but every Person may comprehend these Instructions, if he reads them with Care and Attention, and selects occasionally such Articles as may serve to direct him, as a Rule, in whatever he undertakes. These Instructions ought to be frequently perused, to render them more familiar: And every one may be firmly assured that they will certainly be understood; because,*

524. Assiduity *and* Care *will* conquer *every* Difficulty; *as, on the* Contrary, Indolence *and* Carelessness *will* deter *from every laudable Attempt.*

525. *To render this difficult Affair more easy; these Instructions are to be read over once, at the Beginning of every Month, in the Commission for composing the New Code of Laws, and in all the subordinate Committees, which depend upon it; particularly the respective Chapters and Articles intrusted to their Care, till the Conclusion of the Commission.*

526. *But as no perfect Work was ever yet composed by Man; therefore, if the Commissioners should discover, as they proceed, that any Rule for some particular Regulations has been omitted, they have Leave, in such a Case, to report it to Us, and to ask for a Supplement.*

The Original signed with Her Imperial Majesty's *own Hand, thus,*

Moscow, *July* 30 1767

Catherine

2   *A Critical Contemporary Russian View of Catherine II's Innovations*

The chief beneficiaries of the transformation of Russian socie-ty during the reign of Catherine II were the Russian nobles who, for the most part, fully approved her innovations. There were, however, a few nobles who were critical of her policies. The most prominent of these critics were A. N. Radishchev, N. I. Novikov, and Prince M. M. Shcherbatov. Because Catherine II punished Radishchev and Novikov soon after they voiced their objections to her policies, they influenced their countrymen more posthumously than they did during their lifetimes. Shcherbatov escaped her censorship because his criticism was not published until 1896 (or one hundred years after Catherine II's death), and also because he was a more influential man than were his two unfortunate contemporaries.

A woman not born of the blood of our sovereigns, who deposed her husband by an armed insurrection, she received, in return for so virtuous a deed, the crown and sceptre of Russia, together with the title of 'Devout Sovereign', in the words of the prayer recited in church on behalf of our monarchs.

It cannot be said that she is unqualified to rule so great an Empire, if indeed a woman can support this yoke, and if human qualities alone are sufficient for this supreme office. She is en-dowed with considerable beauty, clever, affable, magnanimous and compassionate on principle. She loves glory, and is assidu-ous in her pursuit of it. She is prudent, enterprising, and quite well-read. However, her moral outlook is based on the modern philosophers, that is to say, it is not fixed on the firm rock of God's Law; and hence, being based on arbitrary worldly princi-ples, it is liable to change with them.

SOURCE. Prince M. M. Shcherbatov, *On the Corruption of Morals in Russia.* Edited and Translated with an Introduction and Notes by A. Lentin (Cam-bridge, England: Cambridge University Press, 1969), pp. 235–259 (alternate pages). Reprinted by permission of Cambridge University Press.

In addition, her faults are as follows: she is licentious; and trusts herself entirely to her favourites; she is full of ostentation in all things, infinitely selfish, and incapable of forcing herself to attend to any matters which may bore her. She takes everything on herself and takes no care to see it carried out, and finally she is so capricious, that she rarely keeps the same system of government even for a month.

For all that, once on the throne, she refrained from taking cruel vengeance on those who had previously vexed her. She had with her her favourite, Grigory Grigor'evich Orlov, who had helped her to accede to the throne. He was a man who had grown up in alehouses and houses of ill-repute. He had no education, and had hitherto led the life of a young reprobate, though he was kind and good-hearted.

This was the man who reached the highest step which it is possible for a subject to attain. Amid boxing-matches, wrestling, card-games, hunting and other noisy pastimes, he had picked up and adopted certain rules useful to the state. His brothers did likewise.

These rules were: to take vengeance on no one, to banish flatterers, to leave each person and government-organ in the uninterrupted execution of their duties, not to flatter the monarch, to seek out worthy men and not make promotions except on grounds of merit, and finally, to avoid luxury. These rules were kept by Grigory Grigor'evich Orlov (later Count and finally Prince) to the day he died.

Finding that gambling can bring others to ruin, he gave it up. Although Counts Nikita and Pyotr Ivanovich Panin were his sworn enemies, he never did them the least harm; on the contrary, on many occasions, he did them favours, and defended them from the monarch's wrath.

He not only forgave Shvanvich, the man who treacherously attacked his brother, Alexei Grigor'evich, but even did him favours. The many flatterers who tried to exploit his pride, were never successful; on the contrary, it was easier to gain his affection by outspokenness than by flattery. He never interfered with the administration of any government-organ which did not belong to him; and if he did make a request on someone's behalf, he was never angry if his request was turned down. He never flattered his sovereign, for whom he had a genuine zeal, and would tell her the whole truth with a certain outspokenness, and always moved her heart to mercy, as I myself witnessed on many occasions. He liked to seek out worthy men as far as he was able, but he disliked making promotions except on the grounds of merit —this, not only in the case of those whom he benefitted for their worth alone, but even in the case of his boon-companions; and the first sign of his favour was to force a man to serve the nation with zeal and to employ him in the most dangerous situations, as he did in the case of Vsevolod Alexeevich Vsevolozhsky, whom he took with him to Moscow during the Great Plague, and whom he set to work there.

Although he had been dissolute and luxurious in his youth, there was later no trace of luxury to be seen in his house; his house contained nothing exceptional by way of furnishings; his table could not compare with those of the epicures; there was nothing extraordinary about his carriages, though he was fond of horses and racing; and, finally, at no time in his life did he ever wear gold or silver on his clothes.

But all his good qualities were overshadowed by his licentiousness. He scorned his duty to his sovereign and the monarch's Court, and turned the Royal Court into a den of debauchery. There was hardly a single maid-in-waiting at Court who was not subjected to his importunings—and how many of them were weak enough to yield to them!—and this was tolerated by the monarch. Finally, he ravished his thirteen-year-old cousin, Ekaterina Nikolaevna Zinov'ev, and although he later married her, he did not thereby conceal his vice, for he had already publicly revealed his action, and by the marriage itself he broke every law of church and state.

However, during his period of favour, affairs were quite well conducted, and the monarch, imitating her favourite's simplicity, was indulgent to her subjects. There were not many distributions of largesse; duties were carried out, and the monarch's pleasure served instead of rewards. Men were not insulted by being passed over when it came to awarding ranks, and the monarch's pride was often quelled by the truthfulness of her favourite.

However, since virtue is not as prone to imitation as vice, the praiseworthy sides of his conduct were little followed. Seeing the licentiousness of Orlov and his brothers, women prided themselves in striving to become their mistresses, and decency and modesty, already impaired in the time of Peter III, were completely extinguished by long habit during the Orlovs' period of favour, the more so since this was also a means of acquiring the monarch's favour.

His removal, rather than fall, from the position of favourite, gave others the chance to take his place at the side of the licentious Empress, and it may be said that each favourite, however brief his period of favour, has put Russia in debt to the tune of millions of roubles by some vice or other (apart from Vasil'chikov, who did neither good nor evil). Zorich introduced the custom of immoderate gambling; Potyomkin—love of power, ostentation, pandering to all his desires, gluttony and hence luxury at table, flattery, avarice, rapaciousness, and it may be said, all the other vices known in the world, with which he himself is full and with which he fills his supporters, and so on throughout the Empire. Zavadovsky brought base Malorussians to office; Korsakov increased brazen licentiousness among women; Lanskoy made cruelty a mark of honour; Ermolov did not succeed in doing anyting, but Mamonov is introducing arbitrariness in the distribution of ranks and favouritism for his own kinsmen.

The Empress herself, selfish woman that she is, wishes, it seems, to increase the power of vice, not only by her own example, but by her actual encnouragement of it. Fond of glory and ostentation, she loves flattery and servility.

Among her entourage is Betsky, a man of small intellect, but sufficiently cunning to deceive her. Knowing her love of glory, he established many institutions, such as the Foundlings' Homes, the Convent for Young Ladies, the reorganized Land Cadet Corps and the Academy of Arts, and the Loan and Orphans' Bank. In this he behaved like the architect of Alexandria who built the Pharos; on which building he fashioned in alabaster the name of Ptolemy, the king who provided the money for the building; but beneath the alabaster he carved his own name in marble, so that when with the passage of time the alabaster fell away, his name alone should be visible.

So Betsky too, though he made it seem that everything he did was for the glory of the Empress, yet not only does his name appear as chief founder of all his schemes, which have been printed in various languages, but he did not even leave the monarch the power of choosing the directors of these institutions, but he himself was supreme director in every one of them, that is, until his credit collapsed.

And in order to hide this, all methods were used by him in order to flatter her: her praises were sung everywhere, in speeches, in writings and even in ballets performed at the theatre. Once, at a performance at the Cadet Crops of the ballet "The Battle of Chesme," I myself heard her say to me: *"Il me loue tant, qu'enfin il me gâtera."*

She would have been fortunate if a change of heart had accompanied these words, but no, when she said this, her soul was drunk with pomp and flattery.

Ivan Perfil'evich Elagin took no less pains in order to flatter her in public and in private. He being Director of the Court Theatre, various works were written in her honour; her deeds were celebrated in ballet-dances; sometimes "Fame" announced the arrival of the Russian fleet in the Morea, sometimes the battle of Chesme was celebrated; sometimes "The Soldiery" danced with Russia.

Prince Alexander Alexandrovich Vyazemsky, a man of small intellect, but extremely cunning, also used a most artful means of flattery, being Procurator-General and holding in his hands the state revenues. He pretended to be stupid, he pointed out to her the excellent administration of the state perfected under her rule, and said that he himself was stupid, and that everything that he did was on her instructions and under her inspiration. Sometimes he not only compared her wisdom with that of God but said that it was greater; by this means he gained the upper hand over her.

Bezborodko, her secretary, now already a Count, a member of the College of Foreign Affairs, High Chamberlain and Postmaster-General, makes it an invariable rule as far as the administration is concerned, never to contradict her, but to praise and carry out all her orders. For this he has received an immoderate number of awards.

Flattery having reached such a peak at Court among men employed in affairs of state, people have begun to flatter in other ways. If anyone builds a house with money partly given by her or that he has stolen, he invites her to the housewarming, where he writes the following words in illuminations: "A Gift to You from Your Subjects"; or else he inscribes on the house: "By the Generosity of Catherine the Great," forgetting to add: "But to the Ruination of Russia." Or else, festivals are given in her honour, gardens are built, with impromptu spectacles and decorations, everywhere showing flattery and servility.

To add to the corruption of women's morals and of all decency, she has set other women the example of the possession of a long and frequent succession of lovers, each equally honoured and enriched, thus advertising the cause of their ascendancy. Seeing a shrine erected to this vice in the heart of the Empress, women scarcely think it a vice in themselves to copy her; rather, I suppose, each thinks it a virtue in herself that she has not yet had so many lovers!

Although she is in her declining years, although grey hair now covers her head and time has marked her brow with the indelible signs of age, yet her licentiousness still does not diminish. She now realizes that her lovers cannot find in her the attractions of youth, and that neither rewards, nor power, nor gain can replace for them the effect which youthfulness can produce on a lover.

Trying to conceal the ravages of time, she has abandoned her former simplicity in dress, and though in her youth she disliked cloth-of-gold, and criticized the Empress Elisabeth Petrovna for leaving a wardrobe large enough to clothe a whole army, she herself has started to show a passion of her own for inventing suitable dresses and rich adornments for them, and has thus given rise to the same luxury, not only in woman but also in men.

I remember, when I entered the Court in 1768 there was only one coat in the whole Court that was embroidered in gold—a red cloth coat, belonging to Vasily Il'ich Bibikov. In April 1769, the Empress was angry with Count Ivan Grigor'evich Chernyshov for arriving at Czarskoe Selo on her birthday in an embroidered coat; but in 1777 when I retired from Court, everyone wore clothes of cloth-of-gold with embroidery even on ordinary days, and were now almost ashamed to have embroidery only on the edge of their garments.

It cannot be said that the Empress is particular about food; on the contrary, it may be said that she is too moderate. But her former lover, who has remained her all-powerful friend, Prince Grigory Alexandrovich Potyomkin, is not merely particular aboud food, but a positive glutton. The negligence of the High Marshal of the Court, Prince Nikolai Mikhailovich Golitsyn, in neglecting to prepare some favourite dish of his, subjected him to Potyomkin's vile abuse, and forced him to retire. From this let everyone judge whether it is not a fact that Prince Golitsyn's successors, Grigory Nikitich Orlov and Prince Fyodor Sergeevich Boryatinsky, are not now making every effort to satisfy this all-powerful glutton. And certainly the royal table has become much more magnificent and is far better today.

And also, in order to please this friend of the monarch, people everywhere have begun to try to increase magnificence at table (though it was sufficient even before his time), and this disease of luxury and the desire to glut oneself on the finest fare has spread from the highest to the lowest.

Generally speaking, women are more prone to despotism than men; and as far as she is concerned, it can justly be averred that she is in this particular a woman among women. Nothing can irritate her more than that when making some report to her, men quote the Laws in opposition to her will. Immediately the retort flies from her lips: "Can I then not do this irrespective of the laws?"

But she has found no one with the courage to answer that she can indeed, but only as a despot, and to the detriment of her glory and the nation's confidence. Many law-suits attest to her arbitrariness: (1) the restoration to Mar'ya Pavlovna Naryshkin by Talyzin of certain estates, which has been confirmed as his property by the title-deeds and by actual possession; (2) the case of the children of Prince Boris Vasil'evich Golitsyn concerning the wrongful confiscation of the estates of their grandfather, Streshnev; although this injustice was recognized by the Senate, and a report was submitted requesting permission for them to be restored to the rightful heirs, and although the postscript on the report "So be it" seemed to indicate that their claim was being justly satisfied; yet later the explanation came from the Empress's study that the words "So be it" meant "Let them remain confiscated".

Akim Ivanovich Apukhtin reported to her through the College

of War about the retirement of a certain Major-General; he received the order that the man was to be retired without promo-
tion. When he began to point out that the Laws specifically laid
it down that Major-Generals were to be promoted upon retirement, he received the answer that 'She was above the Laws, and
did not choose to grant him this reward'.

Such examples, seen in the monarch herself, certainly encourage the grandees to similar arbitrariness and injustice, and Russia,
groaning from such outrages, shows daily signs of how infectious
the monarch's example is.

Such an attitude of mind, and particularly in a person devoted
to her favourites, naturally brings with it bias and injustice. I
could supply many examples of both of these; but it is sufficient
if I tell how, because of her dislike of Sakharov, on the grounds
of his immorality (though he had long been her valet-de-
chambre and had enjoyed her confidence, though he was no better then) his case was placed in the archives without consideration. As if immorality was to be punished in a property-suit, a
case in which even a dissolute man may be in the right, and
where the point at issue is not morals and character, but purely
and simply—who owns what.

Then there was the case of Wachtmeister, concerning the
wrongful confiscation of his grandfather's estates in Livonia.
Though his case was upheld by all the departments of the Senate, the verdict he received was that, since the estates had been
already given to General Browne, they should remain his property. Count Roman Larionovich Vorontsov, an avowed bribe-taker
all his life, was appointed Viceroy of Vladimir, where he did not
cease to practice his usual corruptions. These did not escape the
notice of the monarch, but she merely rebuked him with an am-
biguous hint, by sending him a large purse. Only when he was already dead and the people's ruin had gone to extremes, was the
order given for an inquiry into his conduct and that of the governor; and although the people's ruin had lasted seven years, the
inquiry was only authorized to cover two years.

Do not such examples, which are of frequent occurrence, encourage the citizens to indulge in similar conduct for their own
advantage? I have read in a certain book the following clear
symbol: that it is vain to try and draw a true circle when the

centre is uncertain and wavering; the line of the circle will never meet exactly; there are also the words of the Holy Writ, which also clearly signify the duty of those in authority: 'Teacher, Reform Thyself!'

Is it possible to imagine that a monarch who makes such large distributions of largesse, a monarch who is the main recipient of the treasures of the entire state, could be avaricious? Yet so it is; for what else can I call the introduction of that habit, so much censured by all political writers, the habit of selling offices for money? There are many examples of this: the dissolute and avaricious leaseholder, Lukin, having donated 8,000 roubles to the Court out of his ill-gotten gains, and presenting them in the cause of a school for the common people, received the rank of Captain. Then there was Prokofy Demidov, who was almost brought to the scaffold for his lampoons. Though he had been under investigation for the crime of attacking a secretary of the College of Justice in his own house, and though he was responsible for incessant outrages and practical jokes, offensive to any well-constituted government, yet, for donating money to the Foundlings' Home (and thereby insulting his own children), he received the rank of Major-General; and for donating 5,000 roubles in the cause of public education, gratitude was expressed to him publicly in the newspapers. As if the monarch could not establish useful institutions without taking money from corrupt men, and as if dissolute morals could be attoned for with money!

This example has become even more infectious than the others. All offices can be bought, official positions have begun to be given not to those most worthy, but to those who pay most for them, and even these men, once they have paid, have started to recoup their loss by exacting bribes from the people.

Merchants, enriched by peculation of state property, have received high rank; for example, Loginov, a leaseholder, who not only robbed through his leases, but was actually convicted for embezzlement of commissariat funds, received civil rank. Faleev, who as purveyor to the monarch always charged three times too much, has not only received civil rank and a title of nobility for himself, but has also had all his minions promoted to the ranks of staff officer.

Trade has fallen into disrepute, and unworthy men have been

made nobles, thieves and rascals have been rewarded, dissolute-
ness encouraged, and all this before the eyes of the monarch and
with her connivance. Is it possible, then, in view of this, to expect justice and impartiality from the ordinary magistrates?

The whole reign of this monarch has been marked by events
relating to her love of glory. The many institutions founded by
her apparently exist for the good of the nation. In fact they are
simply symbols of her love of glory, for if she really had the nation's interest at heart, she would, after founding them, have also
paid attention to their progress. But she has been content simply
with their establishment and with the assurance that she will be
eternally revered by posterity as their founder; she has cared
nothing for their progress, and though she sees their abuses she
has not put a stop to them.

This is attested by the establishment of the Foundlings' Home,
the Convent for the Education of Young Ladies of the Nobility,
the reorganization of the Cadet Corps, and so on. In the first of
these, a large number of infants have died, and even today, after
over twenty years, few or hardly any artisans have emerged. In
the second, the young ladies have emerged with neither learning
nor morals, apart from what nature has provided them with, and
their education has consisted in acting comedies rather than in
the improvement of their hearts, morals and reason. From the
third, the pupils have emerged with little knowledge and with an
absolute aversion to all discipline.

The wars that have been started attest to this still more. Pon-
iatowski was raised to the Polish throne out of favouritism; it
was wished to provide him with an autocratic form of government, contrary to the Polish liberties. The protection of the Dis-
sidents was undertaken; and instead of striving to invite these
victims of religious persecution to join their co-religionists in
Russia, and thereby to weaken Poland and strengthen Russia,
occasion was given for a war with Turkey, fortunate in its events,
but costing Russia more than any previous war. The Fleet
was sent to Greece and under God's protection won a victory; but the only motive behind this expedition was love of glory. Poland has been partitioned, thereby strengthening the houses of Austria and Brandenburg, and losing Russia her powerful
influence over Poland. The Crimea has been acquired, or rather,

stolen, a country which, because of its difference of climate, has proved a graveyard for Russians.

Measures have been drawn up which men are not ashamed to call laws, and the new provincial governorships have been filled indiscriminately, to the ruin of all that went before, to the detriment of society, to the increase of sharp practice and the ruin of the people; and no watch is kept over these governors to see whether they carry out their instructions exactly.

Laws have been concocted, called Rights of the Nobility and Municipal Rights, which contain a deprivation rather than a granting of rights, and lay a universal burden on the nation.

Such an unbridled love of glory is also encouraging the growth of an enormous number of large buildings everywhere. Farmers have been attracted away from their land by the prospect of greater employment and gain; yet the state revenues scarcely suffice for such buildings, which even when built, will be a burden to maintain. Private men, too, are copying this passion, founded on love of glory, that their names, inscribed on a building, should survive for many centuries, and have plunged madly into the erection of such buildings and their decoration.

One man, out of affluence, will spend many thousands of roubles in building houses, gardens and summer-houses for his comfort and pleasure; a second does the same out of ostentation, and a third, following this pernicious example, does the same in order not to fall behind the others, and spends beyond his means. All three, though they may find themselves comfort and pleasure, are gradually brought to ruin by this luxuriousness. They become a burden to themselves and the state, and often make up their losses by bribe-taking and other deplorable means.

My conscience assures me that all my descriptions, however black they may be, are unbiased; truth alone and the corruption into which all my fellow-subjects have fallen and from which my country groans, have compelled me to commit them to paper. And so, from a fair description of the morals of the Empress, it is quite possible to see the disposition of her heart and soul.

True friendship has never resided in her heart, and she is ready to betray her best friend and servant in order to please her lover. She has no maternal instincts for her son, and her rule with everyone is to cajole a man beyond measure and respect him as long as he is needed, and then in her own phrase 'to throw away a squeezed-out lemon'.

Examples of this are as follows: Anna Alexeevna Matyushkin, who was always loyal to her even during her period of oppression, was finally banished. Count Alexei Petrovich Bestuzhev, who had helped her when she was Grand Duchess in all her designs, and had suffered misfortune on her behalf, was deprived of all her trust at the end of his life, and after his death she reviled him. Count Nikita Ivanovich Panin, who had helped her to accede to the throne, saw all his offices taken away from him in his old age, and perhaps it was this that brought about his death. Nikolai Ivanovich Checherin, who served her with all possible zeal and enjoyed her favour, was in the end so victimized by her that he ended his life prematurely.

Prince Alexander Mikhailovich Golitsyn, the Field Marshal, the silent executor of all her orders, died without any regret on her part; for though the news of his death was known in the morning, yet that day she went merrily to a concert, and, having indulged her merriment, asked her lover, Lanskoy, on the way out, how Prince Alexander Mikhailovich was; and on receiving the news of his death, she then pretended to burst into tears; this certainly shows, incidentally, what a false heart she has. Countess Praskov'ya Alexandrovna Bruce, who was long her favourite and friend, was finally banished from Court, and died of grief. Let each judge from this whether pure sentiments of friendship can abide in the subjects after such examples.

Having painted this sad picture, I do not think I need to state whether she has faith in God's Law, for if she had, then God's Law itself might improve her heart and set her steps on the path of truth. But no: carried away by her indiscriminate reading of modern writers, she thinks nothing of the Christian religion, though she pretends to be quite devout.

However much she conceals her thoughts, these are frequently revealed in her conversation, and her deeds prove it even more. Many books by Voltaire, undermining religion, have been translated by her order, such as *Candide, The Princess of Babylon,* and others; and Marmontel's *Belisaire,* which makes no distinction between pagan and Christian virtue, was not merely translated by a society at her order, but she herself took part in translating it.

And her tolerance of, or rather, permission for unlawful marriages, such as those of Princes Orlov and Golitsyn with their cousins, and of General Bauer with his step-daughter, proves this most of all. And so it may be said that even this indestructible bastion of conscience and virtue has been destroyed in her reign.

X. CONCLUSION

By such stages Russia has reached the ruination of all good morals, which I mentioned at the very beginning. A deplorable situation. We must only beg God that this evil may be eradicated by a better reign. But this cannot be until we have a monarch who is sincerely attached to God's Law, a strict observer of justice, beginning with himself; moderate in the pomp of the royal throne, rewarding virtue and abhorring vice, showing an example of assiduity and a willingness to take the advice of wise men; firm in his undertakings, but without obstinacy; gentle and constant in friendship, showing an example in himself by his domestic harmony with his wife, and banishing licentiousness; generous without prodigality at his subjects' expense, and seeking to reward virtue, good qualities and merit, without any bias, able to delegate his tasks, able to distinguish those which the monarch must take upon himself and those which belonged to the various departments of state, and finally, possessing sufficient magnanimity and patroitism to draw up and hand on fundamental laws for the state, and firm enough to carry them out.

Then exiled virtue, leaving the deserts will enthrone herself amid the cities and at the Court itself. Justice will not tilt her scales whether for bribery or for fear of violence; fear and corruption will be banished from the grandees; patriotism will ensconce itself in the hearts of the citizens. Men will boast, not of luxurious living and riches, but of impartiality, merit and disinterestedness. They will not reckon who is in or out of favour at Court, but with law and virtue as their object, will consider them as a compass, able to lead them to both rank and fortune. The nobles will serve in various offices with a zeal proper to their calling; merchants will cease to aspire to be officers and noblemen; each will keep to his own class, and trade will flourish with the decrease in the import of foreign goods which give rise to voluptuousness, and with the export of Russian goods. Arts and crafts will increase so as to produce within Russia whatever is needed for the luxury and magnificence of a certain number of people.

3   A Critical Contemporary Foreign View of Catherine II's Russia

During the reign of Catherine II, similarly as during that of Peter I, thousands of Western Europeans came to Russia for temporary or permanent settlement. For whatever reasons they may have come, many Western Europeans left interesting accounts of their impressions of the great changes that were taking place in Russia at that time. Some were very complimentary; others were very critical. One of the most interesting of these accounts is by Frenchman Charles François Philibert Masson (1762-1807), a full-time writer and a part-time diplomat, who spent a number of years in Russia observing with a keen eye and recording with trenchant sharpness both the virtues and vices of Russian society.

The character of Catherine can, in my opinion, only be estimated from her actions. Her reign, for herself and her Court, had been brilliant and happy; but the last years of it were particularly disastrous for the people and the Empire. All the springs of government became debilitated and impaired. Every general, gover-

SOURCE. [Charles François Philibert Masson], *Memoirs of the Court of St. Petersburg . . .* (Philadelphia: George Barrie & Son, 1898) , pp. 56–74, 79–81, 83–87, 308–310, 319–321, 343–349. Spellings, especially of proper names, have been modernized.

nor, chief of department, was become a petty despot. Rank, justice, impunity, were sold to the highest bidder. An oligarchy of about a score of knaves partitioned Russia, pillaged, by themselves or others, the finances, and shared the spoils of the unfortunate. Their lowest valets, and even their slaves, obtained in a short time offices of considerable importance and emolument. One had a salary of from three to four hundred rubles a year (£30 or £40) which could not possibly be increased by any honest dealing, yet was he sufficiently rich to build round the palace houses valued at fifty thousand crowns (£12,500). Catherine, so far from enquiring into the impure source of such sudden wealth, rejoiced to see her capital thus embellished under her eyes, and applauded the inordinate luxury of these wretches, which she erroneously considered as a proof of the prosperity of her reign. In the worst days of France, pillage was never so general, and never so easy. Whoever received a sum of money from the Crown for any undertaking, had the impudence to retain half, and afterwards complained of its insufficiency, for the purpose of obtaining more; and either an additional sum was granted, or the enterprise abandoned. The great plunderers even divided the booty of the little ones, and thus became accomplices in their thefts. A minister knew almost to a ruble what his signature would procure to his secretary; and a colonel felt no embarrassment in talking with a general of the profits of the army, and the extortions he made upon the soldiers. Every one, from the peculiar favourite to the lowest in employ, considered the property of the State as a harvest to be reaped, and grasped at it with as much avidity as the populace at an ox given up to be devoured. The Orlovs, as well as Potemkin and Panin, filled their places with a degree of dignity. The first displayed some talents, and an inordinate ambition. Panin had greater genius, greater patriotism, and more virtues. In general, during the last years of Catherine, none were so little as the great. Without knowledge, without penetration, without pride, without probity, they could not even boast that false honour which is to loyalty what hypocrisy is to virtue; unfeeling as bashaws, rapacious as tax-gatherers, pilfering as lackeys, and venal as the meanest Abigails of a play, they might truly be called the rabble of the Empire. Their hirelings, their valets, and even their relations, did not accumulate wealth by the gifts of their bounty, but by the extortions committed in their name, and the traffic made of their credit; they also were robbed themselves, as they robbed the Crown. The meanest services rendered to these men were paid by the State, and the wages of their buffoons, servants, musicians, private secretaries, and even tutors of their children, defrayed out of some public fund, of which they had the control. Some few among them sought for talents, and appeared to esteem merit; but neither talents nor merit acquired a fortune under their protection, or partook of their wealth; partly from the avarice of those patrons, but still more from their total want of decency and judgment. The only way of gaining their favour was by becoming their buffoon, and the only mode of turning it to account was by turning knave.

Thus, during this reign, almost every man in office, or who had credit at Court, was the favourite of fortune, and acquired riches and honours. At the galas given by the Empress, swarms of new-created counts and princes made their appearance, and that at a time when in France all titles were about to be abolished. If we except the Saltikovs, we shall find at this period no family of distinction taken into favour. To any other country this would have been no evil; but in Russia, where the rich nobility is the only class that has any education, and often any principles of honour, it was a serious calamity to the Empire. Besides, all these upstarts were so many hungry leeches, who must be fed with the best blood of the State, and fattened with the hard earnings of the people. A frequent change of kings is often not burdensome to a State, to whom it still remains an inheritance; but a continual change of favourites and ministers, who must all load their hives before they depart, is enough to ruin any country but Russia. How many millions must it have cost to fill successively the rapacious maws of about a dozen peculiar favourites? How many to render rich and noble the Bezborodkos, the Zavadovskys, the Markovs, and a too numerous list of others who might be named? Have not the Orlovs, the Potemkins, the Zubovs, acquired revenues greater than those of kings; and their underlings, agents in the sale of their signatures, and managers of their petty traffic, become more wealthy than the most successful merchants?

With respect to the government of Catherine, it was as mild and moderate within the immediate circle of her influence as it was arbitrary and terrible at a distance. Whoever, directly or indirectly, enjoyed the protection of the favourite, exercised, wherever he was situated, the most undisguised tyranny. He insulted his superiors, trampled on his inferiors, and violated justice, order, and the *ukazes*, with impunity.

It is to the policy first, and next to the weakness of Catherine, that the relaxed and disorganized state of her internal government must, in part, be attributed; though the principal cause will be found in the depraved manners and character of the nation. How was a woman to effect that which the active discipline of the cane, and the sanguinary axe of Peter I. were inadequate to accomplish. The usurper of a throne, which she was desirous to retain, she was under the necessity of treating her accomplices with kindness. A stranger in the empire over which she reigned, she sought to remove everything discordant, everything heterogeneous, and to become one with the nation, by adopting and even flattering its tastes and its prejudices. She often knew how to reward, but never how to punish; and it was solely by suffering her power to be abused that she succeeded in preserving it.

She had two passions, which never left her but with her last breath—the love of man, which degenerated into licentiousness; and the love of glory, which sank into vanity. By the first of these passions, she was never so far governed as to become a Messalina, but she often disgraced both her rank and her sex; by the second she was led to undertake many laudable projects, which were seldom completed, and to engage in unjust wars, from which she derived at least that kind of fame which never fails to accompany success.

The generosity of Catherine, the splendor of her reign, the magnificence of her Court, her institutions, her monuments, her wars, were precisely to Russia what the age of Louis XIV. was to Europe; but, considered individually, Catherine was greater than this Prince. The French formed the glory of Louis; Catherine formed that of the Russians. She had not, like him, the advantage of reigning over a polished people; nor was she surrounded from infancy by great and accomplished characters. She had subtle ambassadors, not unskilled in the diplomatic art, and some fortunate generals; but, Ruminatsev, Panin, and Potemkin excepted, she could not boast a single man of genius; for the wit, cunning and dexterity of certain of her ministers, the ferocious valour of a Suvorov, the ductile capacity of a Repnin, the favour of a Zubov, the readiness of a Bezborodko, and the assiduity of a Nicholas Saltikov, are not worthy of being mentioned as exceptions. It was not that Russia did not produce men of merit; but Catherine feared such men, and they kept at a distance from her. We may conclude, therefore, that all her measures were her own, and particularly all the good she did.

Let not the misfortunes and abuses of her reign give to the private character of this Princess too dark and repulsive a shade! She appeared to be thoroughly humane and generous, as all who approached her experienced. All who were admitted to her intimacy were delighted with the good-natured sallies of her wit. All who lived with her were happy. Her manners were gay and licentious; but she still preserved an exterior decorum, and even her favourites always treated her with respect. Her love never excited disgust, nor her familiarity contempt. She might be deceived, won, seduced, but she would never suffer herself to be governed. Her active and regular life, her moderation, firmness, fortitude, and even sobriety, are moral qualities which it would be highly unjust to ascribe to hypocrisy. How great might she not have been, had her heart been as well governed as her mind! She reigned over the Russians less despotically than over herself; she was never hurried away by anger, never a prey to dejection, and never indulged in transports of immoderate joy. Caprice, illhumour, and peevishness, formed no part of her character, and were never perceived in her conduct. I will not decide whether she were truly great, but she was certainly beloved.

Imbued from her youth with the corrupt maxims by which Courts are infected; enveloped on her throne in a cloud of incense, through which it was hardly possible for her to see clearly, it would be too severe to apply at once the searching light of reason to her character, and try its defects by so strict an inquest. Let us judge her now as we would some twenty years ago, and consider Russia still, as to the people, as in the age of Charlemagne. The friends of liberty ought to render to Catherine the same justice as is rendered by all rational theologians to those great and wise men who did not enjoy the light of revelation. Her crimes were the crimes of her station; not of her heart. The terrible scenes of Ismail and of Prague appeared to her Court to be humanity itself. She needed, perhaps, only to be unfortunate to have possessed the purest virtues; but the unvaried prosperity of her arms dazzled and corrupted her. Vanity, that unfortunate rock, so fatal to every female, was her great failing; and her reign will ever bear the distinguishing characteristic of her sex.

Meanwhile, in whatever light she is considered, she will ever be placed in the first rank among those who, by their genius, their talents, and especially their success, have attracted the admiration of mankind. Her sex, giving a bolder relief to the great qualities she displayed on the throne, will place her above all the examples of real history; and the fabulous ages of an Isis and a Semiramis must be resorted to to find a woman who has executed, or rather undertaken, such daring projects.

The ten last years of her reign carried her power, her glory, and, perhaps, her political crimes, to their height. When the great Frederick, dictator of the Kings of Europe, died, she was left the senior Sovereign, the eldest of the crowned heads of the Continent of Europe; and, if we except Joseph and Gustavus, all those heads taken together were unequal to her own; for she surpassed them as much in understanding as she exceeded them in the extent of her territories. If Frederick was the dictator of these Kings, Catherine became their tyrant. It was then that the end of that political thread by which poor Europe had been moved like a puppet, and which had escaped from France to Berlin, and from Berlin to Vienna, became fixed in the hands of a woman who drew it as she pleased. The immense Empire, an Empire almost of romance, which she had subjected to her sway; the inexhaustible resources she derived from a country and a people as yet in a state of infancy; the extreme luxury of her Court, the barbarous pomp of her nobility, the wealth and princely grandeur of her favourites, the glorious exploits of her armies, and the gigantic views of her ambition, threw Europe into a sort of fascinating admiration; and those Monarchs, who had been too proud to pay each other even the slightest deference, found no humiliation in making a lady the arbiter of their interests, the ruling power of all their measures.

But the French Revolution, so unfriendly to sovereigns in general, was particularly so to Catherine. The blaze which suddenly emerged from the bosom of France as from the crater of a burning volcano, poured a stream of light upon Russia, vivid as that of lightning; and injustice, crimes and blood were seen where before all was grandeur, glory and virtue. Catherine trembled with fear and indignation. The French, those sweet heralds of her fame, those flattering and brilliant historians, who were one day to transmit to posterity the wonders of her reign, were suddenly transformed into so many inexorable judges, at whose aspect she shuddered. The phantoms of her imagination were dispelled. That Empire of Greece she was so desirous of reviving, those laws she would have established, that philosophy she intended to inculcate, and those arts which she had patronized, became odious in her sight. As a crowned philosopher, she valued the sciences so far only as they appeared the instruments for disseminating her glory. She wished to hold them as a dark lantern in her hand; to make use of their light as should suit her convenience; to see without being seen. But when they dazzled her all at once with their bright emanations, she wished to extinguish them. She who had been the friend and disciple of the French speculative writers, now wished to be re-enveloped in the ages of barbarism, but her wishes were vain, the light was not to be resisted; if she composed herself to sleep on laurels, she awoke on the carcases of the dead; Glory, which in illusion she embraced, was changed in her arms into one of the Furies, and the Legislatrix of the North, forgetting her own maxims and philosophy, was no longer anything more than an old sybil. Her dastardly favourites, everywhere pointing out to her in this event, Brutuses, Jacobins, and incendiaries, succeeded in filling up the measure of her suspicions and terrors. Her delirium was even carried so far that, on a King who extended his prerogatives, and a nobility that ameliorated its government, she bestowed the appellations of rebels and traitors; the Poles were treated as Jacobins, because they had not the misfortune to be Russians. . . .

Catherine never effectually patronized letters in the states of her Empire. It was the reign of Elizabeth that had encouraged them; and it was distinguished by many productions worthy of proving to Europe that the Russians may lay fair claim to every species of excellence. Catherine, indeed, purchased a few libraries and collections of pictures, pensioned a few flatterers, flattered a few celebrated men, who might be instrumental in spreading her fame, and readily sent a medal or a snuff box to a German writer who dedicated some hyperobolical work to her; but it was necessary to have come from some distance to please her, and to have acquired a great name to be entitled to her suffrage, and particularly to obtain any recompense. Genius might be born at her feet without being noticed, and still more without being encouraged; yet, jealous of every kind of fame, and especially of that which Frederick the *Unique* had obtained by his writings, she was desirous of becoming an author, that she might share in it. She accordingly wrote her celebrated *Instructions for a Code of Laws;* several moral tales and allegories for the education of her grand-children; and a number of dramatic pieces and proverbs, which were acted and admired at the Hermitage. Her great undertaking, of which she was so vain, of collecting a number of words from three hundred different languages, and forming them into a dictionary, was never executed.

Of all her writings, her letters to Voltaire are certainly the best. They are even more interesting than those of the old philosophical courtier himself, who sold her watches and knitted stockings for her; and who repeats in his letters the same ideas and compliments in a hundred different forms, and excites her continually to drive the Turks out of Europe, instead of advising her to render her own subjects free and happy. If the Code of Laws drawn up by Catherine bespeak a mind capable of enlarged views and a sound policy, her letters announce the wit, graces, and talents of a woman of still greater merit, and lead us to regret the means by which she obtained the acquisition of her power.

When she published her Instructions, all Europe resounded with her applause, and bestowed upon her already the title of Legislatrix of the North. Catherine ordered deputies to be assembled from the different nations of her vast empire; but it was only that they might hear this celebrated performance read, and that she might receive their compliments; for as soon as this was done, they were all sent back to their distant homes, some in disgrace for their firmness, others decorated with medals for their servility. The manuscript was deposited in a magnificent case to be exhibited to the curiosity of strangers. A sort of committee was nominated to reduce these laws into form; and if a favourite or minister had any dependent for whom he wished to provide, or any buffoon whom he wanted to maintain free of expense, he was appointed a member of this committee, whence he derived a salary. Yet all Europe vociferated that Russia had laws, because Catherine had written a preface to a Code, and had subjected a hundred different people to the same system of slavery. . . .

If we except the travels of the celebrated Pallas, the historical researches of the industrious Müller, and some other works upon natural history, no literary production worthy of being noticed has distinguished Russia during the reign of Catherine. Natural history and mathematics are the only sciences which the Russians have contributed in some measure to advance; and even those, however trifling, have been by the help of Germans; yet no country is so fortunately situated for rendering the sciences the most essential services. Natural and ancient history might expect from her the most astonishing discoveries. The ruins of twenty cities attest that Tartary and Mongolia were once inhabited by polished nations, and the monuments which are still being discovered would have realized the sublime conceptions of Buffoon and Bailli. Whole libraries have been discovered under the ruins of Ablai-Kitt, and amid the ruinous heaps that skirt the Irtish. Thousands of manuscripts in unknown languages, and many others in the language of the Chinese, the Kalmyks, and the Manchus, are perishing in the mouldy, deserted cabinets of the academy: had they remained under the ruins till a government or people less barbarous had brought them to light, they would have been better preserved. . . .

Previous to the death of Catherine, the monuments of her reign resembled already so many wrecks and dilapidations: codes, colonies, education, establishments, manufactories, edifices, hospitals, canals, towns, fortresses, everything had been begun, and everything given up before it was finished. As soon as a project entered her head, all preceding ones gave place, and her thoughts were fixed on that alone, till a new idea arose to draw off her attention. She abandoned her code to drive the Turks out of Europe. After the glorious peace of Kainardzhi, she appeared for awhile to attend to the interior administration of her affairs, but all was presently forgotten, that she might be Queen of Tauris. Her next project was the re-establishment of the throne of Constantine: to which succeeded that of humbling and punishing the King of Sweden. Afterwards the invasion of Poland became her ruling passion; and so imperiously did it fascinate her, that a second Pugachev might have arrived at the gates of St. Petersburg without inducing her to relinquish her hold. She died, still meditating the destruction of Sweden, the ruin of Prussia, and mortified at the success of French republicanism. Thus was she incessantly led away by some new passion still stronger in its influence than the preceding one, and thus neglected her government, both in its whole and its parts.

Medals have been struck in honour of numerous buildings which have never yet been constructed; and, among others, the marble church, which, undertaken some twenty years ago, is still on the stocks. The shells of other edifices, which have never been finished, appear like so many ruins; and St. Petersburg is encumbered with the rubbish of a variety of large mansions fallen to decay before they have been inhabited. The projectors and architects have pocketed the money; and Catherine, having the plan or medal in her cabinet, concluded the undertaking to be finished, and thought of it no more.

The St. Petersburg Almanac gives a list of upwards of two hundred and forty towns founded by Catherine—a number inferior, perhaps, to what have been destroyed by her armies; but these towns are merely so many paltry hamlets, that have changed their name and quality by an *immennoi ukaz,* or supreme order of Her Imperial Majesty: some of them even are nothing more than posts driven into the ground, containing their name, and delineating their site; yet, without waiting till they shall be finished, and particularly till they shall be peopled, they figure on the map as if they were the capitals of so many provinces.

Prince Potemkin has actually built some towns, and constructed some ports, in the Crimea. They are fine cages, but they have no birds; and such as might be allured thither would shortly die of chagrin if they had not the power of flying away. The Russian Government is subjugating and oppressive; the Russian character warlike and desolating. Tauris, since it was conquered, has become a desert.

This mania of Catherine to sketch everything and complete nothing, drew from Joseph II. a very shrewd and satirical remark. During his travels in Tauris, he was invited by her to place the second stone of a town, of which she had herself, with great parade, laid the first. On his return, he said, "I have finished in a single day a very important business with the Empress of Russia: she has laid the first stone of a city, and I have laid the last." . . . .

Russia offers an example truly singular in the annals of history. The same century has seen five or six women reign despotically over an Empire, in which the women before were slaves to men who were themselves enslaved; where Peter I. was obliged to employ force to raise them out of this barbarous state of debasement, and give them a place in society; where even now the code of slavery does not allow them a soul, or count them among human creatures. The reigns of these females afford a strong argument in favour of those nations who have never suffered the sceptre to be placed in hands that were formed for the distaff, for it would be difficult to find six reigns more prolific in wars, revolutions, crimes, disorders, and calamities of every kind. That the manners of the Court were softened I am ready to allow; but then they were corrupted, and wretchedness increased in equal proportion with luxury and disorder. Abuses of every kind, tyranny and licentiousness, became the very essence of government.

The old proverb, "When women hold the sceptre, men guide it," is false or unmeaning. When women reign their lovers tyrannize over the people, and all in power plunder them. But, without entering into the political effects of petticoat government, which may well be considered as the extreme of baseness or extravagance in mankind, I shall notice only the influence it has had on society and the female sex in Russia.

The existence of the Amazons appeared to me no longer a fable, after I had seen the Russian women. Had the succession of Empresses continued, we might perhaps have seen that nation of female warriors locally reproduced, and in the same clime where they formerly flourished. Great energy is still observable in the women of the Slavic nations, of which their history furnishes many proofs. That feminine activity, which love, tenderness and domestic cares absorb in other countires, the women of the North, who are born with more cold and robust constitutions, employ in search of sway and in political intrigue. They frequently experience a physical necessity of inspiring love, but their hearts seldom feel a want of returning it. . . .

Almost all the ladies of the Court kept men with the title and office of favourites. I do not say lovers, for that would imply sentiment; while theirs was merely gross desire, or, frequently, a wish to follow the fashion. This taste was become as common as eating and drinking, or dancing and music. Tender intrigues were unknown, and strong passions still more rare. Debauchery and ambition had banished love. Marriage was merely an association, in which convenience alone was considered; it was fortunate if friendship sometimes came, unsought, to lighten the chains which the interest of parents, or vanity alone, had formed.

The discovery of a society, called the Club of Natural Philosophers, made a few years ago at Moscow, completely proves the depravity of tastes and manners under the reign of Catherine. This was a kind of order, surpassing in turpitude everything related of the most immodest institutions and mysteries. The men and women, who were initiated, assembled on certain days, to indulge promiscuously in the most infamous debaucheries. Husbands introduced their wives into this society, and brothers their sisters. The novices were not admitted till they had been examined and gone through their probations; the women being admitted by the men, the men by the women. After a sumptuous feast, the company were paired by lot. When the French Revolution took place, the Russian police were directed to examine and dissolve all kinds of orders and assemblies, and on this occasion the Club of Natural Philosophers was examined, and its members were obliged to disclose its mysteries. As the members of both sexes belonged to the most wealthy and powerful families, and their assemblies had nothing to do with politics, nothing more was done than to shut up and prohibit their scandalous lodge. . . .

The Russians in general, following the example of their latter Sovereigns, had for some time endeavoured to emerge from barbarism, and attended to the education of their children with much care. To bestow on them knowledge and talents was formerly the happy means of bringing them into notice, and procuring them advancement. They spared neither pains nor expense to cultivate the arts and sciences in a country where these were strangers, as they force fruits to ripen in their winter gardens and hothouses. Elizabeth and Catherine founded several institutions in favour of youth, some of which, as the Normal Schools, and particularly the three different corps of cadets, presented the interesting sight of several thousand young men educated at the expense of the State, and taught morality, languages, sciences and arts. Those are now either abolished or suffered to fall to decay.

The convent of young ladies, though the sentiments from which it was founded were worthy of the generosity of a great Princess, has completely failed of its end, like most of the other institutions. Two or three hundred young women of no fortune receive here an excellent education; but, as soon as they reach the age of eighteen, they are turned out of doors. They enter into a world from which they have lived secluded since their infancy; seldom find either relations, or any who know them; and are ignorant whither to turn. In consequence, they fall victims to the officers of the guards, whose barracks surround the convent, and who watch every term of dismission to ensnare the prettiest. It would be very practicable to save, out of the immense cost of their education, a sufficient sum to portion them, or, at least, to keep them till they were provided for.

The education of those young Russians who have some fortune is commonly entrusted to private governors, known and decried in Russia by the name of *uchiteli,* "teachers." Most of them are foreigners, chiefly French or Swiss. The Germans, in spite of their good qualities and pedagogical erudition, differ too widely in character from the Russians, to rival them; and the trials which some have wished to make of their own countrymen from the University of Moscow, or from the schools of St. Petersburg, have not given satisfaction. . . .

The *uchiteli,* whom some endeavour to ridicule, and others consder as dangerous, have contributed more than any others to polish Russia, as they have given instruction in detail, man by man. They are the only people whose office has been to preach philosophy, virtue and morals, while diffusing knowledge. To begin with the celebrated le Fort, who inspired Peter I. with the desire of gaining knowledge, and end with a petty clerk of some French attorney, who teaches his pupils to conjugate a few verbs in his own tongue, the *uchiteli* have been the persons who have communicated to the Russians that taste, those acquirements, and those talents, for which many of them are admired in foreign countries. No doubt it is to be lamented that, among the number of those who devote themselves to private tuition, and make it their trade to form men, there are so many unworthy of the employment, whose ignorance and immorality bring ridicule and odium on their colleagues. But such tutors begin to find it difficult to obtain situations, except in remote country places, where some honest Russians of the old stamp fancy they have bestowed a good education on their children, when they hear them speak a foreign language. At St. Petersburg people were become more difficult in the choice of tutors, and among them were to be found persons of real merit. They were the only class of men in Russia, without excepting the Academicians, who cultivated literature and the sciences, which they did in some degree. A Brueckner, in the house of Prince Kurakin; a Grammont, at the Princes Dolgoruky's; a Lindquist, an Abbé Nicole, and several others, without having places equally advantageous, were worthy of the profession to which they devoted themselves, and were distinguished for their success as much as for their merit.

The great men of Russia, who have much wealth and high posts, are too ignorant, or too much engaged in gaming and intrigue, to interfere with the education of their children; and as colleges and universities are wanting in that country, they pursue a very prudent plan. As soon as they have made choice of the man who is to supply their place in the duties of a father, they confer on him great power and confidence; the most intelligent could not do better, were they discerning in their choice. It is seldom that a governor is so destitute of sense, information and honour, as to abuse his functions; he feels himself most happily disposed towards his pupil; to instruct him, form him, acquire his attachment, and gain his love, are the wishes of his heart. If he be in a worthy, opulent house, he has no occasion to regret the sacrifice of ten or twelve years of his life, as he will be provided for. In his pupil he often finds a real friend, and always a protector. His own interest prompts him to inspire his pupil with just and noble sentiments, and to give him a taste for the sciences; which is far more important, and far more difficult, than to teach him the elements of them. Thus, most of the young Russians pass their early days with a foreigner, who becomes their second father, and for whom they retain a due sense of gratitude if they are in the least well born.

This education by means of foreigners has one peculiar effect. Almost all the Russians, being educated by Frenchmen, contract from their infancy a decided predilection for France. With its language and history they are better acquainted than with their own; and as, in fact, they have no country, France becomes that of their heart and imagination. . . . Besides they learn to know France only in the most pleasing aspect, as it appears when at a distance. They are taught to consider it as the country of taste, politeness, arts, delicate pleasures, and amiable men; as the asylum of liberty, as the altar of that sacred fire at which the torch may one day be kindled to illumine their benighted country. The French emigrants, driven to the territories of the modern Cimmerians, were astonished to find there men better acquainted than themselves with the affairs of their own country; but these were young Russians who had read, and meditated on what they read, from Rousseau and Mirabeau; the emigrants had read nothing, and brought nothing with them but their prejudices. Many young Russians were better acquainted with Paris than those who had spent their lives in roaming about its streets. It has in general been remarked that the Russians have the most happy dispositions, and a surprising readiness of conception; whence they make a very rapid progress in everything that is taught them. There are no children more amiable or more interesting; many, when their domestic education is finished, have acquired more select and extensive knowledge than other young men who have frequented the German universities; and they have particularly a wonderful readiness at displaying their knowledge on seasonable occasions. Too frequently, however, these are precocious flowers, that produce no fruit; they seldom travel like an Anacharsis; and their return to their own country usually puts an end to their studies, and even to their taste for science and literature.

4   *An Assessment of Catherine II's Reign by a Prerevolutionary Russian Historian*

Generally speaking, before 1917 Russian historians praised Catherine II's foreign policy (mainly because of her successful wars of conquest and territorial expansion) and criticized her domestic measures (mainly because of her punishment of her critics and her extension of serfdom). An exception to this rule was the eminent Russian historian Vladimir Stepanovich Ikonnikov (1841–1923) author of a monumental four-volume work on Russian historiography, who, in his analysis of Catherine II's reign, emphasized the positive and the relevant aspects and, accordingly, deemphasized the sensational and erotic elements in her life.

During Elizabeth's reign the dominant influence in education, literature and the theater was French. People with means organized French libraries and engaged French governors and governesses for their children, while others went to study in Paris (Count A. M. Efimovskii, Count A. R. Vorontsov). At the age of 12, Count A. R. Vorontsov was quite familiar with the works of Racine, Corneille, Boulle, Voltaire, and others. Princess E. R. Dashkova (his sister) wrote: "As soon as I started reading (she was born in 1744) books became the object of my concern: Bayle, Montaigne, Boulle, and Voltaire were my favored authors." Elizabeth's favorite, I. I. Shuvalov, regularly received the latest literary news from France; N. I. Panin and M. L. Vorontsov had libraries; while Dashkova already in her early life assembled a 900-volume library that included the French Encyclopedia and a dictionary by Moreri.

By her education Catherine belonged to this group. . . . Her frequent trips (to Braunschweig, Zerbst, Kiel, Hamburg, Berlin,

SOURCE. V. S. Ikonnikov, *Znachenie tsarstvovaniia Ekateriny II* [The Significance of Catherine II's Reign] (Kiev: 1897), pp. 3–5, 9–10, 12–14, 16, 24–27, 39–40, 49–55, 60–63, and 65–66. Translation by Basil Dmytryshyn.

and other places) enabled her to develop a sense of observation and character. Count Hillenborg, a Swedish nobleman, while in Hamburg, noted that the young Catherine was not developed physically, but had the mind of a philosopher. Five years later (in 1745) he saw her in Russia and directed her attention to the reading of serious books, especially Plutarch's *Lives,* a biography of *Cicero,* and Montesquieu's *The Greatness and the Decadence of the Romans.* A copy of the latter was found with some difficulty in Petersburg and she read a part of it. Then followed Brantome's *Works; The Life of Henry IV,* by Péréfixe; *A History of Germany,* by Barre; Plato's *Works;* Voltaire's *Universal History*; Bayle's *Historical and Critical Dictionary;* Montesquieu's *Spirit of the Laws; Church Annals,* by Baronius (which were translated during the reign of Peter the Great) ; *Annals,* by Tacitus, and Sévigné's *Letters.* "During 18 years of boredom and solitude (1744–1762) I willy-nilly read many books," Catherine subsequently wrote. But when she started reading Voltaire's works, novels ceased to interest her. She also read Rebelais, Scarron, Montaigne; Moliere and Corneille. Her favored was Lesage, the author of *Gil Blas.* The works of these writers contained the best of the old French sharpness. . . .

At about the time when she started corresponding with Voltaire, Catherine also established contacts with d'Alambert, whom she invited to educate Grand Prince Paul Petrovich (in 1764 d'Alambert was elected an honorary member of the Academy of Sciences) along with Diderot, whose Encyclopedia served her as a reference work, and where she hoped to find everything she needed. She suggested that its [the Encyclopedia's] publication be completed in Riga. A work by Helvetius, *De l'homme,* was published in 1773 in London by her special envoy Prince D. A. Golitsyn, and was dedicated to her by the publisher. Catherine bought Diderot's library (in 1765) but left it for his use till his death and paid him 50,000 livres to be her librarian. "What times we live in," wrote Voltaire to Diderot, "France persecutes philosophy while the Scythian supports it!" He called Catherine one of the brightest of stars of the North "because all other stars would let Diderot starve." "The three of us—Diderot, d'Alambert and I are building altars for you; you have turned me into a heathen. We all are now missionaries who spread the faith of St. Catherine, and we can say proudly that our faith is quite widespread," he noted. Catherine's friends succeeded in stopping the publication of a history of the 1762 events, written by Roulle. Voltaire called those events a petty family affair unworthy of attention. . . .

One of her intermediaries with the Encyclopedists was Prince D. A. Golitsyn; Betskii corresponded with Diderot and Geoffrin; Count A. P. Shuvalov and Count A. R. Vorontsov with Voltaire and Marmontel; Ivan A. Shuvalov and Prince Iusupov visited with Voltaire; Prince Kozlovskii considered it a special honor to be sent by Catherine to Ferney; Grimm accompanied Field Marshal Rumiantsev's sons to do homage to Voltaire. Prince G. G. Orlov invited Rousseau to his estate and K. G. Razumovskii searched for Rousseau in Strasbourg. Dashkova was twice in Paris (1770 and 1780), had lengthy talks with Diderot, and visited with Voltaire at Ferney. P. S. Potemkin translated the works of Voltaire and Rousseau, while Admiral Greig studied the works of Montesquieu and Raynal. In 1772 Catherine wrote Voltaire that many officers who had visited with him were enthusiastic about their reception, and that the young longed to see him again and to listen to his talk. Poroshin called the works of Montesquieu and Helvetius to the attention of Grand Prince Paul Petrovich. . . .

Obviously the spread of ideas of contemporary philosophy was not without results. Catherine was proud that Russia received the works that were prohibited by the Sorbonne and the Papacy, and that some of those works could even be found in Siberia! In 1765 Voltaire published his *Philosophy of History* which, according to Kazanova, sold 3,000 copies in Russia within one week (?). People carried it in their pockets as a prayer book and those of the high society even swore by Voltaire's name. In the library of a foundling hospital were works of Descartes, Puffendorf, Locke, Voltaire and many others, and Betskii punctually sent new copies of the Encyclopedia. Catherine selected the work by Bilfeld (a member of the Berlin Academy of Sciences) for the education of her son and also to be used in the Cadet Corps. With others (in 1767), she helped to translate Marmontel's book *Bélisaire,* a bold protest against intolerance. She herself translated Chapter 9 in its entirety, wherein autocracy is subjected to a trenchant criticism. She later wrote a letter to the author himself. The translation of Marmontel's book was entrusted to Gavriil, Bishop and later Metropolitan of Tver. Deputies to the Legislative Commission based themselves on the principles of natural law, and contract theory, and civil equality. Lectures were given at Moscow University on the connection between legislation and philosophy (in 1766); on the need to establish a judicial system based not on antiquated views or rules but on sound judgment, for the benefit of society. Torture was criticized (in 1767); and lectures on the theory of law (in 1782–3), followed the ideas of Montesquieu. Such Russian historians as Prince Shcherbatov and Boltin adopted the views of French and English writers (Voltaire, Montesquieu, Hume and others) to Russian history. Shcherbatov also considered the problem of freedom of conscience and capital punishment similarly as did contemporary philosophes.

From the beginning of Catherine's reign there was an increased effort to send young people to foreign universities to study political, judicial, natural, and medical sciences, theology, and foreign languages. (Between 1763 and 1795, 36 students studied at Leipzig; 5 at Göttingen from 1766 to 1772; 2 at Oxford; 4 at Glasgow; 2 at Uppsula; 2 at Köningsberg; 15 at Kiel from 1766 to 1789; and several studied medicine in Paris). Between 1784 and 1787 44 Russian and Lifland [Baltic region] students studied at the University of Strasbourg. Also sent abroad were officers sailors, artists, and even children of merchants to study trades. At the Empress' initiative, a special commission was established in 1768 to translate works from foreign languages into Russian. From her own funds Catherine gave the commission 5,000 rubles annually. Russian literature was greatly enriched by translations from Greek and Roman authors as well as from the most outstanding contemporary writers in various branches of learning.

Following the example of Mme. de Epinay, Catherine opened her own Hermitage, renowned for its literary works, library, and art collections. She acquired the paintings, prints, and cameos of Teniers, Wouwerman, and Vanloo. The famed Mangs painted pictures for her; Reifenstein made copies of the famous works of Raphael, which now form a precious property of the Imperial

Hermitage. She succeeded in securing the services of architect Guarenghi, the portrait painter Lampi, and the composer Sarti. She was interested in the discoveries at Pompei, and supported Russian artists. . . .

After she ascended the throne Catherine paid attention to Lomonosov, and on June 7, 1764 she visited his home, inspected his mosaic works, and watched his experiments in physics and chemistry. Thanks to her personal intervention, Schlötzer commenced his work at the Academy and later became an eulogist and a chronicler of her reign. She opened the archival material to Müller, Shcherbatov, Novikov, and Golikov, who published a great amount of source material. Count A. I. Musin-Pushkin, known for his collection of manuscripts, was also greatly indebted to Catherine II. She saw to it (in 1781 and 1793) that Russian chronicles and literary monuments were gathered, from monastery and church libraries, for publication, and during her reign Russian chronicles were first published in such great quantities that subsequently they were not published for quite some time. At the Archive of the College for Foreign Affairs (in Moscow) an attempt was made to describe Russia's relations with foreign powers. A number of collections and journals containing material on history and ethnography of Russia also appeared. . . .

Another vital act of her administration was the founding in Petersburg (in the middle of 1765) of the Free Economic Society which was sponsored by the Empress herself. Its primary aim was to cater to agricultural interests, the foundation of the country's prosperity. Similar societies existed in Scotland, Ireland, England, Germany, Switzerland and France. The Russian society [Free Economic Society] was founded ahead of that of Austria and Prussia. Among its participants were several courtiers, high administrators, members of the Academy of Sciences and the College of Medicine, professors, and writers. The society started the publication of its works, sent out questionnaires on agriculture to provinces, established premiums, and prepared information on Russia for inclusion in the Encyclopedic Lexicon. Catherine herself selected the most important task for the society: to determine "what is more beneficial for a society—for peasants to have the right of land ownership or to have only the right to movable property, and how far should this right extend on either of the propositions." 162 responses were received to that question from various parts of Europe, primarily in the German language, and seven in Russian. The first prize went to Bearde de l'Abbe, member of the Dijon Academy, whose composition was published alongside several others in the 1768 *Works* of the Society. . . .

It is well known what kind of destruction smallpox once created. Emperor Peter II died from its effects, and Catherine tells us how terrified she was during the epidemic of 1767. She became interested in smallpox vaccination and invited from England Dr. Dimsdale, who performed several experiments in the Cadet Corps, in private homes, and then vaccinated the Empress, Grand Prince Paul, and many inhabitants of the capital. She received congratulations for it, and ordered that a commemorative medal be struck . . . In St. Petersburg, Moscow, and other cities, even in Siberia, smallpox committees and clinics were opened. The death caused by smallpox of an heir to the Spanish throne (in 1771), and then of Louis XV in 1774, induced Catherine to say in a letter to Voltaire and Grimm "how shameful it is that so many people should die of smallpox in the eighteenth century; that is simply barbarism! . . . ."

From the first day of her reign, Catherine decided to give the country new laws. She was influenced in this by the example of earlier legislative commissions, by personal knowledge of the problem, and by studying leading contemporary works in the field—namely those of Montesquieu and Beccaria. She hoped to resolve that problem with the aid of deputies from the entire empire "in order to learn best about the situation in each district." The result of her personal interest in this matter was the famed *Nakaz* whose ideas were subjected to a twofold modification: by her close advisors and by the members of the Legislative Commission. It was published subsequently. Catherine did not conceal that "she selected Montesquieu as President of her Empire without naming him. He loved mankind so much that he will not be offended by it; his book is my prayer book," she added. Actually about 250 articles of the published *Nakaz*, out of 526, were taken from Montesquieu's *Spirit of the Laws,* and about 100 from Beccaria's work. . . .

The Commission had at its disposal a considerable amount of material from Russian and foreign legislative acts, beginning with the Russian translation of the Magna Carta of King John. The Commission also had access to the views of well-known writers and publicists. Catherine suggested that Marshal Bibikov use the *Journal* of the English Parliament as a guide in preparing exerpts from daily transactions for publication. . . .

The Legislative Commission, the Gubernia Reform Act, and other Charters, influenced public life and activity. According to Boltov, Catherine's reforms "caused great intellectual excitement, forced all nobles to think, to act, and to be concerned." He says that this period was "doubtless the most memorable in Russia's modery history, and that by its impact it caused great changes everywhere." Other contemporaries (Dashkova, Dobrynin, Prince Th. N. Golitsyn, Vinskii) point out to the improvement of city administration, roads, trade, education and manners. The publication of government decrees, the introduction of new institutions, the election of officials, the opening of new administrative departments, the celebration of peace—all were accompanied by meetings of all officials and by the gathering of local nobles from the neighboring gubernias. These gatherings were often well attended (in Novgorod about 650, in Tver about 500). . . .These gatherings were accompanied by fireworks, masquerades, theatrical performances, etc. Those attending did not limit their participation to eating, drinking, and playing, but expressed interest in the unfolding events. They talked a great deal about them and were quite excited. It is obvious that when they returned home they carried with them many "new impressions," new ideas, and new topics for conversation and contemplation.

Theaters appeared not only in Petersburg and Moscow, where spectacles were organized in private homes, but also in provincial towns (Voronezh, Kharkov, Tula, Kaluga, and others; attempts were made to organize spectacles in Irkutsk and even in villages of some nobles). . . .

During Catherine's reign educational institutions presented the following picture. In 1787 there were 165 schools with 11,157 attending; in 1796 there were 316 schools with 17,341 attending. Catherine valued the educational activity of the Jesuits, whom she allowed, similarly as did Frederick II [of Prussia], to stay in Russia and take part in popular education in Belorussia [that part of Russia acquired in the three partitions of Poland]. "To tell the truth," she wrote to Grimm, "these monks are exceptional people. No one has been able to duplicate the schools they have even though many have tried to plagiarize their ideas."

During Catherine's reign the following schools were independently established: a school for the children of merchants, founded in Moscow in 1772 with the financial support of P. A. Demidov; a Mining School, founded in 1774 with a broad curriculum and well-trained personnel that started a work on compiling a Mining Dictionary, and that operated a printing press until 1795; a Greek Gymnasium (or a Cadet Corps) established in 1775; and, a school for land surveyors established in Moscow in 1779 (later renamed Surveying Institute). In 1785 the Artillery, the Engineering, and the Page Corps were reorganized along the pattern adopted by the Land Corps, whose commandant from 1789 to 1794 was the famed pedagogist Count Anhalt. In 1783 the curriculum at the Smolny Institute was expanded to conform with the plan of "regular education." New medical schools were established: in 1783 in Petersburg at the Kalinkin Hospital, and in Elisavetgrad at a hospital founded by Potemkin in 1788. In 1787 medical schools were separated from hospitals; their curricula became theoretically oriented, and they became known as Medical-Surgical Schools . . . An agricultural school was founded in Nikolaev, and interest began to develop in improving agriculture and utilizing coal deposits in the south of Russia. In 1789 an Asian school was started in Omsk. . . .

Moscow university attracted many Russian professors, and in 1767 lecturing in Russian became obligatory. Lectures were strongly influenced by the ideas of the Universities of Göttingen and Glasgow (through Tretiakov and Desnitskii), and also those of Adam Smith and Kant. The latter was elected an honorary member of the Academy of Sciences in 1794. The University's Medical School received the right to grant doctors' degrees to its medical students. There were organized at the University such societies as: The Free Russian Assembly, the Learned Friendly Society, and the Society of the Admirers of Learning. The first of these published a journal, *Opyt trudov,* (from 1774 to 1783), where a number of articles and sources on Russian history appeared. In their lectures, professors discussed problems that interested the government (vaccination, health, education, etc.) and some took part in translating the leading works of scientific literature. . . .

In 1766, after lengthy and intense requests, Catherine succeeded in bringing the famous Euler from Berlin to Petersburg Academy of Sciences, where until his death in 1783 he continued his scholarly research that resulted in a number of works. Several students (Kotelnikov, Rumovskii, Kraft, Fuss, and others) studied under his supervision. Euler's three sons served in Russia. Russian members of the Academy of Sciences (Kotelnikov, Ozeretskovskii, Kononov, Zakharov and others) delivered public lectures on mathematics, physics, chemistry, and natural history. In its Russian language publications, the Academy acquainted the Russians with scientific achievements in the West, and gave a prominent place to works on Russian history and literature.

Between 1768 and 1774 four scientific expeditions were organized (two to Orenburg and two to the Astrakhan region) by members of the Academy and other individuals (Pallas, Gmelin, Hildenstädt, Lepekhin, Faulk, Zuev and others). They gathered and published much material on diverse problems of Russia which has not lost its value to the present time. One of the participants in the expedition, Georgy, published (1776–1780) in German a work entitled *A Description of All Nations Inhabiting Russia* (3 parts and an Appendix) with many drawings. It was later translated into Russian and French. Academician Lacksman studied the natural history of Siberia.

In 1769 Russia took an active part for the second time (the first was in 1761) in observations associated with the passage of the planet Venus before the sun. For that purpose three expeditions were sent to Lapland, one to Iakutsk, and several observers were dispatched to the Urals. The Empress took part in the observations in Oranienbaum. In 1783, based on the French example, the Russian Academy of Arts and Letters was organized to work on the Russian language and to prepare a dictionary (between 1789 and 1794 five volumes were published). . . .

The field of art was not forgotten. At the end of Catherine's reign her Hermitage included, not counting paintings and reproductions of Raphael, about 10,000 prints and drawings, and 10,000 cameos. The office of natural history occupied two large rooms. The library had 38,000 volumes. Catherine deserves credit for many of Petersburg's outstanding buildings. . . .

Naturally the literary outlook of Catherine was quite broad. She knew the works of Tasso and Milton, Locke and Newton, Rousseau and Abbot St. Pierre, Richardson and Fielding, Stern and Algarotti. She read Homer in Stolberg's translation, and Shakespeare in Eschenburg's translation. . . . Catherine's close contacts with the leading thinkers of the West found reflection in Russian literature. From the start of her reign lengthy translations of Voltaire's works into Russian were undertaken. Most appeared in the 1770's and 1780's in individual volumes or in sets. Over sixty titles of his works appeared. In 1789 the publication in Moscow of all of his translated works was suggested, but this project was not realized. Translated also were the works of Montesquieu, Diderot, d'Argens, Mercier, Helvetius, Maupertuis, Rousseau, d'Alambert, Buffon, Condillac, Marmontel, Mably, Hume, Robertson, and others. In 1767 Kheraskov published in Moscow a collection (3 volumes) of *Translations from the Encyclopedia;* Bolton translated the Encyclopedia up to the letter "K"; and Verevkin wanted to translate the entire Encyclopedia. Russian readers could at that time read in their own language Rousseau's *On the Inequality Among Men* (1770); a project by Abbot St. Pierre entitled *On Universal and Eternal Peace* (1771) ; Hobbes' *On Citizenship* (1776) ; and Thomas More's *Utopia* (1789). Many "Voltarians" appeared within Russian society (Karin, Rakhmaninov, Prince Gorchakov, Kartsov, Opochinin, Kliushin). Not only among the cultured aristocrats, but also among the middle classes spread published works and manuscripts of the above leading figures as evident from contemporary memoirs and literary pieces . . . Education was often carried out in the same spirit. A son of Count A. S. Stroganov (a friend of Emperor Alexander I) was from 1779 on educated under the guidance of Guilbert Romme, subsequently one of the most active members of the Convention; Lesage, later Secretary of the Geneva Revolutionary Committee, lived in P. A. Tolstoy's home; a Prussian named Brückner, a pure Voltairian, lived at the Kurakins' home; while Marat, brother of a leader of the Convention, who later changed his name to de Bourdy, stayed at V. P. Saltykov's home. . . .

Many outstanding writers appeared during this time. What is vital to note is that literature responded to the important problems that Catherine either touched upon herself or that were associated with her reign. Catherine knew how to inspire love in literature and in individuals who surrounded her (Count Orlov, Potemkin, Lanskoi and others) and who tried to cater to her tastes. Her state secretaries were excellent stylists and took an active part in her own literary works and in drafting governmental decrees. The translated literature of the period acquainted its readers with the best works of English and French belletristics (moral, comedy, satire), civic drama, and comedy—all of which influenced the development of Russian theater. Simultaneously, journalistic activity developed on a large scale. In some Catherine took an active part (*Interlocutor, This and That*). Journals also appeared in provinces (Iaroslav, Tobolsk). Such scholarly publications and collections as *Ancient Russian Library* and its *Supplements; St. Petersburg Scientific News,* etc. appeared. To appreciate properly this literary movement, it is sufficient to say that before Catherine II's reign about 15 periodicals were published in Russia; during her reign that number rose to 90. . . .

Before Catherine II's reign there were few women writers in Russia; the blossoming of their activity took place during her reign. There are known about 70 names of women writers who entered the literary arena during her reign. Contemporaries speak sometimes of these women as "the admirers of free sciences and of arts." Many of them drifted to the milieu of well-known writers or took an active part in contemporary journals. In Tambov a group of women writers revolved around Derzhavin; in Riazan Princess Volkonskaia organized something resembling a literary society, where she delivered a lecture "On the Influence of Women on Fine Arts." Obviously almost all Russian women writers of the eighteenth century were noblewomen. The appointment of Princess Dashkova as the Director of the Academy of Sciences and President of the Russian Academy caused foreigners to remark that women in Russia enjoyed broad powers. No less interesting was the fact that, thanks to Dashkova's insistence, in 1784 the Academy published a book entitled, "On the Nobility and Advantages of Womanhood". . . .

There is no doubt that no person exerted as profound an influence on publishing activity as did N. I. Novikov. As I. V. Kireevskii correctly observed, he did not spread but created the love for books and the urge to read them. According to Karamzin, before Novikov there were only two bookstores in Moscow with annual sales of about 10,000 rubles. Soon there were 20 bookstores with sales of 200,000 rubles. In addition, Novikov opened up bookstores in other, even distant, towns of Russia. He distributed almost cost-free (hence the debt of his press) the works he considered important, and soon not only all of European Russia but Siberia as well began to read. Then Russia, even though for a brief time, witnessed a unique development in the history of her enlightenment, the appearance of *public opinion*. Literary societies and public libraries appeared (Tula, Kaluga) ; there developed, according to Boltov, a passion for newspapers, reading, and a widely circulated manuscript literature. In the homes of nobles there appeared libraries and collections of pictures and prints.

At the end of Catherine's reign a public library in Petersburg was proposed; here also private clubs performed the same service. The appearance of a free public library in Moscow is associated with Novikov's activity.

5   *An Assessment of*
Catherine II's Reign in Soviet Historiography

In Soviet historiography the reign of Catherine II has been portrayed as a classic example of stagnation and corruption by the country's leadership and as a period of great creativeness and rebellion by the masses. Soviet scholars have voiced little or no criticism of Catherine II's successful wars of conquest that

SOURCE. M. V. Nechkina, et al., ed. *Istoriia SSSR s drevneishikh vremen do 1861 g.* [A History of the USSR from Ancient Times to 1861] (Moscow: Gospolitizdat, 1956), Vol. 1, pp. 581–602. Translation by Basil Dmytryshyn.

gained very valuable territories for the Russian empire. Below is a typical example of this kind of analysis. It was prepared for Soviet university students and was published in 1956.

The requirements of economic development of the country and the needs of the state apparatus forced the government to introduce certain measures in the realm of education. But, similarly as in the middle of the eighteenth century, their scope was quite insignificant when compared with the country's needs and the tasks which existed in that realm. At the end of the century only half of the gubernia capitals had secondary schools (gymnasia) and more than half of the uezd capitals did not have even two-year elementary schools.

Equally slowly did the government adopt measures aimed at creating specialized schools and educational institutions to prepare cadres for various branches of the economy and administration. Only the following were opened: a mining school, a land-surveyor school, a commercial school, a medical-surgical academy; while the Engineering and Artillery Corps were reorganized. With the founding of the Smolny Institute for girls of the nobility and of the Catherine Institute for city girls, the beginning was made for the education of women. Yet even after these measures were adopted there were in the entire country only slightly over 300 secondary, elementary, and special schools, and the number of those studying in these institutions barely reached 20,000.

In the educational system the class principle continued to prevail. One of the clearest examples of the reactionary measures of Catherine's government in the realm of education was the introduction of a system of boarding schools where pupils 5 to 6 years old were admitted. The introduction of these educational institutions was based on theories of French educators who advocated "creation of a new species of mankind." In reality this tendency aimed at isolating educational institutions from public life in the country, and educating those attending them in the ultramonarchial and clerical spirit. After she applied this principle to the activity of the Smolny and Catherine Institutes, Catherine sought to spread it to other educational institutions the (Academy Gymnasium, the Academy of Arts, and others) and thereby caused a great deal of harm.

The insignificant number of educational institutions in the country created a situation that induced many nobles to resort to a system, that became quite widespread, of educating their children at home with the aid of foreign tutors. Since the majority of foreigners employed in Russia as teachers were incompetent and without the required skills, the education usually centered in implanting some external luster such as learning of "good manners" and the French language. A typical picture of domestic education of provincial nobility was provided by D. I. Fonvizin in his comedy *Nedorosl* (The Minor).

One of the most important centers of Russian education in the second half of the eighteenth century was Moscow University, opened in 1755, which trained national cadres in the realm of culture and education, and which advocated principles of education and learning which were advanced for those times. The University did not limit its function simply to teaching its own and gymnasium students. It opened broad popularization of knowledge. It regularly sponsored public debates and lectures, prepared and published texts, and published scientific, philosophical, and socio-political literature. In 1756 the university started publishing the first newspaper in Moscow—*Moskovskie Vedomosti*—and later a number of literary journals. In the 1770's the country's first literary-scientific society was founded at the university. Its aim was the publication of vital Russian literary and historical sources and monuments, as well as research in language and literature.

The educational activity of the university became especially significant between 1779 and 1789, when the University press was headed by a well-known publicist, the originator of progressive satirical journalism in Russia, writer and publisher Nikolai Ivanovich Novikov (1744–1818). Because of repressions by Catherine's government, early in the 1770's he was forced to terminate the publication of his anti-serfdom journals, "Drone" and "Painter." After he became head of the University Press, Novikov developed a book publishing and book selling enterprise which was very extensive for those times. He published a number of socio-political, literary, and scientific journals, books on history, geography, and economy of the country, and issued and distributed the leading examples of Russian, as well as foreign, scientific, philosophical, and artistic literature. He published about 1000 titles. His publications, in his own words, were intended not for nobles but primarily for readers "among townspeople and merchants." Novikov did a great deal in acquainting Russian readers with the leading works of West European writers, thinkers, and scholars. He published in Russian the works of Shakespeare, Cervantes, Lessing, Beaumarchais, Molliere, Voltaire, Bacon, Rousseau, Montesquieu, Locke, and others. Novikov gave a prominent place in his journals and other publications to problems of education. He himself advocated progressive pedagogical principles. The leading forces of contemporary Russia centered around Novikov's publishing. His activity had a great progressive significance, in spite of the fact that during his Moscow activity he set aside criticism of the existing system in Russia (which was the basic preoccupation of his satirical journals of the 1760's and 1770's), and concentrated on advocating moral self-perfection. Subjected to constant repressions, seeing no social forces to give him the essential support, and frightened by the peasant war under the leadership of Pugachev, Novikov fell under the influence of Masonic mysticism and alongside educational literature published a number of Masonic books.

Though Novikov was not a revolutionary, his activity greatly disturbed the government of serf owners. After a series of attacks and repressions his press was taken away from him, the bulk of his publications confiscated, and in April, 1792, he was arrested and placed in the Schlüsselburg Fortress. From there he was released four years later a physically and spiritually broken man, and thereafter he took no part in the socio-political and cultural life of the country. The treatment of Novikov and of his publishing house was one of the clearest examples of repressions which the autocracy administered to spokesmen of Russian progressive culture at the end of the eighteenth century.

Science and technology in Russia during the second half of the eighteenth century made significant progress in their development. As a result of expeditions by I. I. Lepekhin, V. F. Zuev, N. Ia. Ozeretskovskii, S. Ia. Rumovskii, P. S. Pallas and others, which the Academy of Sciences organized, rich material on geography, mineralogy, botany, and zoology was assembled. A number of astronomical observations was also carried out and valuable cartographical data were received. In addition, these expeditions provided much valuable data on the country's economy and on the ethnography of Russia's peoples.

In the Academy of Sciences worked V. M. Severgin, a distinguished chemist and mineralogist, and Leonard Euler (1787–1783) a world-renowned mathematician and mechanic who had returned to Russia in the 1760's. While still abroad Euler was the first to recognize the value great inventions by Lomonosov and helped him considerably in his struggle against reactionaries in science.

The publication at the end of the eighteenth century of the first complete dictionary of the Russian language was a major scientific achievement. This work was executed under the leadership of a famous naturalist and philologist, I. I. Lepekhin. It played a tremendous role in the formation and development of the national Russian literary language.

Great successes were also achieved by the developing Russian medicine. The following persons played a vital role in this field: K. I. Shchepin, a prominent surgeon, who first started medical lectures in Russian; D. S. Samoilovich, the founder of Russian epidemiology; and S. G. Zybelin, the first professor of medicine at Moscow University and a first-rate physician. Zybelin paid much attention to causes of diseases, worked fruitfully in pediatrics, and argued that the high rate of mortality in Russia and the slow increase of population was caused by difficult conditions of the enserfed peasantry.

The condition of agriculture and the desire to improve it led to the first steps in the development of Russian agronomy and soil study. At Moscow University, Professor M. I. Afonin prepared a monograph on the origin of chernozem. Vital work in agronomy was also carried on by A. T. Bolotov, and I. I. Komov. With Novikov's help Bolotov began publishing one of the first journals on agronomy in the country. Questions of agronomy, improvement of agricultural implements, cultivation of special crops, etc., occupied a prominent place in publications and works of the Free Economic Society, which commenced its activity in the 1760's. . . .

The development of Russian technology was closely tied with the growth of industry and the needs of city construction, and was closely associated with the creativeness of distinguished Russian inventors who stemmed from the lower strata of the population. The most outstanding were the works of I. I. Polzunov (1730–1766). The son of a soldier, Polzunov, who spent much time in mining, conceived and built at the Kolyvan mine in the Altai the world's first steam engine. He was forced to work in extremely difficult material conditions—a situation that undermined his health. The machine he built was destroyed a year before his death.

No less tragic was the fate of another outstanding self-made inventor, I. P. Kulibin (1735–1818). Son of a townsman from Nizhnii-Novgorod, Kulibin invented a three-wheel cycle (a prototype of the present bicycle), a self-propelled boat, a lamp with a reflector, artificial limbs for invalids, and other things. Kulibin's most outstanding technical creation was a project and model of a one-arch bridge across the Neva River. Unfortunately most of his inventions received no practical application. After he saw his inventions destroyed, Kulibin died in poverty.

In the 1780's a master in the Urals, K. D. Frolov, built the first hydraulic machine. R. Glinkov, a merchant from Kaluga, invented a card for the treatment of flax and a multi-spinning machine. T. I. Voloskov, an inventor from Rzhev, worked on an automatic clock, and was one of the first founders of automation in Russia. In addition, he contributed greatly to the production of native dyes for industry.

The condition and development of technology during this time testified to the developing cleavage between the creative facts and technical achievements of the people on the one hand, and the possibilities of utilizing these inventions in industry on the other. Serfdom ever greatly hindered the development of the country's productive forces and aggravated her backwardness. . . .

The development of art, which was a vital part of national culture, was also closely tied with the socio-economic development of the country as well as with the process of the formation of the Russian nation. The best contemporary works of art reflected democratic, national, and realistic features. Serfs, whose names have in most instances remained anonymous, built mansions and erected other structures in nobles' complexes, adorned their walls with sculptures and paintings, designed sumptuous parks and decorated them with statues and fountains, performed in serf theaters and orchestras, composed musical texts for spectacles and festive occasions, and sang in choirs. Russian craftsmen, working people, and serfs created such beautiful examples of applied art as Gzhel ceramics, Kholmogora [wood] carvings, Vologda lace, china, crystal of Russian manufacture, embroideries, blankets, and jewelry products. The majority of Russian architects, artists, and musicians, who gained fame and recognition in the second half of the eighteenth century, were sons of peasants, craftsmen, soldiers, and petty officials. Their background induced them to express in their works national creativity, realism, and democratic tendencies. . . .

During the second half of the eighteenth century there occurred in the country construction of grandiose Petersburg palaces. Nobles built sumptuous homes and country estates in the vicinity of Petersburg and Moscow. A network of public buildings, in the capital and in major cities, and huge cathedrals were erected. The needs of socio-economic and political development of the country determined the activity of a number of outstanding Russian architects. Their creations expressed boldness, scope of design, and masterly execution.

The dominant trend in architecture of the time was classicism. In contrast to classicism in literature, this classicism embodied progressive and national tendencies. Using forms and examples of ancient architecture, and basing themselves in their creativity on ancient Russian architectural monuments and West European structures, leading [Russian architects of the eighteenth century] created a number of outstanding buildings that were distinguished by clarity, simplicity, and striking combination of monumentality with grace and harmony of remaining parts. The creations of Russian architects of this time are real masterpieces and occupy a prominent place in world architecture. . . .

The first place among Russian architects belongs to the outstanding V. I. Bazhenov (1737–1799) who, in his creations, expressed most clearly the spiritual strength of the people. One of the most beautiful buildings in Moscow, which Bazhenov designed, was Pashkov's home (the old building of the Lenin Library). The apex of Bazhenov's creativity was a grandiose project of the Great Kremlin Court and a complex of Kremlin buildings. He worked on the project for many years, and completed a model and the foundation. The project was unfinished, since Catherine's government terminated financial support. The second outstanding creation of Bazhenov was the Empress' Court near Moscow, which on Catherine's order was destroyed. Catherine's attitude toward Bazhenov was one of hostility.

Simultaneously with Bazhenov worked another major architect—M. F. Kazakov (1738–1813). Many of his creations currently adorn Moscow. These include: the home of Prince V. M. Dolgorukov-Krymskii (the Building of Unions); the Senate (the Building of the Government of the USSR inside the Kremlin); Peter's Court (the N. E. Zhukovskii Academy); the old building of Moscow University; and others.

The famous Russian architect I. E. Starov built the enormous Taurida Palace and the Alexander Nevskii Cathedral in Petersburg. In the center of Petersburg and in its vicinity beautiful structures were designed by such foreign architects as Ch. Cameron and J. Guarenghi, who made Russia their second homeland.

During the second half of the eighteenth century, Russian painting reached outstanding achievement in world art. Since painting of this time was strongly influenced by tastes and demands of clients—who were either aristocrats or nobles—the ideas of freedom and democracy expressed themselves here less clearly than in literature. Nevertheless Russian artists gained outstanding achievements in mastering the technique of painting as well as composition and diversity of content of their works. They gave Russian painting clear national character.

The work of A. P. Losenko, "Vadimir and Rogned", and of G. I. Ugriumov, "The Entry of Alexander Nevskii to Pskov", laid the foundation to Russian historical painting; while the work of S. F. Shchedrin and F. Ia. Alekseev gave birth to landscape painting. In the works of E. P. Chemesov and G. T. Skorodumov, Russian engraving reached high levels.

Especially outstanding were the successes of Russian portrait painters. Following largely the requirements of classicism, Russian artists of the time adopted an independent approach. They centered their attention on the individual's personality, trying to express its qualities and dignity. . . .

Even more than in painting, classicism was clearly expressed in sculpture. The majority of sculptors worked at the time in the decorative field, adorning palaces, parks, and public buildings. Russian sculptors were guided by the experience and achievements of foremost representatives of Western Europe. Many completed their training abroad under the guidance of French and Italian artists. Others worked alongside foreign artists in Russia. Of special significance in the development of monumental sculpture was the work of French sculptor E. M. Falconet, who created a monument to Peter I, known as "The Bronze Horseman". The most noted representatives of Russian classicism were M. I. Kozlovskii, creator of the famous sculpture of Samson in Peterhof and a monument to A. V. Suvorov in Petersburg; I. P. Matros, creator of outstanding tombstones as well as monuments to Minin and Pozharskii in Moscow (1818) and Lomonosov in Archangel. F. F. Shchedrin was also a major artist, creating a number of sculptures for the Admiralty, Peterhof, and the Kazan Cathedral.

F. I. Shubin (1740–1805), the creator of a beautiful gallery of busts, played a vital role in the history of Russian art in the eighteenth century. His works were distinguished by a versatile depiction of features, clear tendencies towards realism, and a wonderful technique. In Lomonosov's bust, Shubin conveyed brilliantly the picture of a wise, bold, and resolute individual, and expressed profoundly the national features of Lomonosov's face. When he depicted the faces of nobles and Tsars, Shubin did not try to idealize them. On the contrary, a number of his busts were interpreted as beautiful satires (the bust of A. A. Bezborodko, that of police commissioner E. M. Chulkov, and the bust, staggering in force and boldness, of Emperor Paul I). The son of a peasant, and a countryman of Lomonosov, Shubin, more than other Russian painters and artists, attained realism and contributed much to its entrenchment in Russian art.

Russian professional theater, established in the middle of the eighteenth century, was considerably behind that of Western Europe with its multi-century history. Nevertheless it developed quite rapidly. A number of outstanding Russian performers appeared. These were: P. A. Plavilshchikov, T. M. Troepolskaia, S. N. Sandunov, and others, who, by their creativeness, implanted into the Russian stage the realism which is associated with the appearance in the nineteenth century of M. S. Shchepkin. In the second half of the eighteenth century the serf-theater was quite widespread. Many gifted representatives of the people performed on its stage. A major opera singer of the time was a serf-girl of Count Sheremetev, P. I. Zhemchugova-Kovaleva.

In the second half of the eighteenth century appeared the first music publications and collections of popular songs. An opera was formed and concerts were started. In music, whose backwardness was very great compared with Western Europe, there began to appear independent features based on a tie with popular creativity. These tendencies appeared in the works of Composer E. I. Fomin, author of a popular comic opera, "The Miller, the Wizard, the Cheater and the Matchmaker," and of the gifted composer-violinist I. E. Khandoshkin, and others.